The Rise and Fall

of Indian Country,

1825–1855

The Rise and Fall
of Indian Country,
1825–1855

William E. Unrau

University Press of Kansas

Published by the University Press of Kansas (Lawrence, Kansas 66045), which was
organized by the Kansas Board of Regents and is operated and funded by
Emporia State University, Fort Hays State University, Kansas State University,
Pittsburg State University, the University of Kansas, and Wichita State University

Library of Congress Cataloging-in-Publication Data

Unrau, William E., 1929–

The rise and fall of Indian country, 1825–1855 / William E. Unrau.

p. cm.

Includes bibliographical references and index.

ISBN 978-0-7006-1511-7 (cloth : alk. paper)

1. Indians of North America—Government relations. 2. Indians,
Treatment of—United States—History—19th century. 3. Forced
migration—Government policy—United States—History—19th century.
4. Land tenure—Government policy—United States—History—19th century.
5. United States—Territorial expansion. 6. United States—Race relations.

I. Title.

E93.U9985   2007

973.5—dc22

2007005004

British Library Cataloguing-in-Publication Data is available.

Printed in the United States of America

10 9 8 7 6 5 4 3 2 1

The paper used in this publication meets the minimum requirements
of the American National Standard for Permanence of Paper for
Printed Library Materials Z39.48-1992.

In memory of
Cleo and Emily

Contents

Maps

Preface

During the course of my preparing the first draft of this book a good friend and his wife came to our home for dinner. As we sipped reasonably good wine prior to one of Millie's delightful oven dinners, my friend rather abruptly inquired of me, "Do you take *National Geographic?*" I admitted outright that I did not but probably would, were it not for the burgeoning national debt, outrageous utility bills, and fears concerning the future of democracy in America and elsewhere. "Your fears are valid and important," he responded, "but what I am telling you right now is more important, for it deals *precisely* with the Indian country business you have been carping about and trying to explain to me for the past several months, actually for more than a year," at which point he ceremoniously handed me a 20" x 31" map entitled "Indian Country."

It was one of those colorful and truly spectacular maps occasionally offered as a supplement to *National Geographic* subscribers, this one dated September 2004. As I was thanking my friend for his generosity I saw the caption on the map he obviously had taken to be right down my professional alley: "What *is* Indian country?" followed by a statement that read in part:

For five centuries the question has been contested on battle-fields, legislated in Congress, and studied in classrooms—yet today the debate burns with a new fire.

The U.S. government generally defines Indian country as the roughly 56 million acres that lie within the boundaries of reservation or other land it recognizes as belonging to American Indians and Alaska natives. But the borders blur under a morass of multiple ownership and conflicts over sovereignty.

Above all else the map provided evidence supportive of my own view that Indian country, at bedrock level dating back to 1825, was simply a place, a physical location where the dispossession and suffering of one culture transpired for the benefit of another. Or, as the editors of the *National Geographic* map stated, a place where land was "transferred from Indians to whites." Coming to my attention at a somewhat difficult time during the composition of this book, the map reinforced my efforts to try to understand what had gone wrong with the government's plan for Indian improvement on the prairie-plains west of Iowa and Missouri during the quarter century prior to 1855.

An unprecedented effort to arrest the taking of Indian land was inaugurated in 1834 when Congress created a special "Indian country" (not "Indian territory," as is sometimes mistakenly written) by law for the so-called emigrant Indians destined to reside, voluntarily or involuntarily, in the trans-Missouri West. Generally viewed as a humanitarian and perhaps well-intentioned law, which, with better enforcement, oversight, and public support, might have saved numerous Indians from an early death while at the same time improving their economic and social status, the endeavor was flawed from the beginning, especially for the numerous so-called indigenous Indians who had sustained themselves without assistance in the trans-Missouri West for at least two centuries prior to the government's

Indian country and removal programs of the 1830s. The sad and destructive result was that a policy of safe haven and permanence proved ineffectual from the start and that Indian country as contemplated and implemented by federal officials (with the support of sundry "friends of the Indian") as an ideal place for Indians was anything but that. How and why this happened, within the context of evolving federal Indian policy, is what I hope to explain in the pages that follow.

A word regarding sources. Even a fleeting glance at the endnotes and sources used in this study suggests that here, one more time, we have history principally based on the records of non-Indians: letters, memos, debates, treaties, statutes, court records, newspaper reports, and travel accounts, mostly supportive of the white presence in Indian country. It is therefore important to note that Record Group 75 ("Records of the Bureau of Indian Affairs"), as well as other Record Groups in the National Archives containing documents dealing with Indian affairs and policy, contain precious few documents indisputably written by Indians without white redaction. To carry such commentary a bit further, it may be appropriate to note also that the first printing press in Indian country, the one placed in operation by Baptist missionary Jotham Meeker among the Shawnees nearly four months prior to the creation of Indian country in 1834, printed Christian hymns in a primitive transliteration of the Shawnee language, not Shawnee complaints about the government's removal program or white interlopers stealing timber from their reservation west of the future Kansas City. Nor did Meeker call attention to bootleggers dispensing alcohol among the Shawnees and neighboring tribes in brazen defiance of federal law.

Here and there, however, the native perspective shines through, as in the case of a letter undeniably written by Potawatomi Chief Quish-Queh-Leh to President Andrew Jackson in 1835, celebrating his tribe's departure from the crowded and wicked East to a new reservation made safe by his Great Father's "strong fence" in the West. The importance of such a document can hardly be overstated; I hope I have used it judiciously, as I have tried with an admittedly much larger number of non-Indian sources.

No historian functions well without the help of others. We quote one another freely, sometimes in a manner not always understood by our critics or general readers. We fret and fume while trying to overcome our biases, and occasionally consult with one another simply to shore up our wavering resolve. With this in mind I am pleased to acknowledge the following persons whose writings and/or professional advice over the years have had a significant impact on my own thinking: Robert G. Athearn, Donald J. Berthrong, Henry F. Dobyns, R. David Edmonds, Paul W. Gates, William H. Goetzmann, William T. Hagan, Joseph Herring, Frederick E. Hoxie, Francis Jennings, James C. Malin, Craig Miner, L. G. Moses, Francis P. Prucha, James P. Ronda, John D. Unruh, Jr., and Elliott West. The analysis and conclusions that follow are, of course, my own.

William E. Unrau
Louisville, Colorado
April 2006

I

Looking Backward

Many, perhaps most, students of Indian-white relations view the Indian Trade and Intercourse Act of 1834 as a central feature of federal Indian policy during the first half of the nineteenth century. Looming large in the development of the government's removal strategy, that is, the removal of eastern Indians to the trans-Missouri West, which had been under consideration for more than a decade, the act of 1834 was a remarkable achievement. Indeed it was, according to a widely cited twentieth-century study, "a milestone in American Indian policy."[1]

Even so, problems persisted after the 1834 law went into effect. Illegal sales of alcohol to Indians continued, leading to devastating socioeconomic conditions for individual Indians and sometimes entire tribes. Indian leadership after 1834 was not always forthright and was on occasion downright corrupt. Federal intervention in intertribal conflicts over land claims between displaced eastern Indian people and their counterparts west of Missouri and Arkansas—and, in fact, in most of the trans-Mississippi West—was minimal at best. Most important of all, however, the demands of white land jobbers for additional tribal terrain indicated that all would not be well in the

Indians' promised land. Yet tribal opposition to removal was less pronounced than in the past. Confusion regarding reservation boundaries in the East and new ones in the West appeared to have been eliminated, and in several important instances the Supreme Court rendered decisions favorable to federal over state authority in the administration of Indian affairs—decisions that in the opinion of most informed Indian leaders constituted the least of several evils. Thus with not a little confidence the Jackson administration could, in the wake of the 1834 act, "commend the nation for what had been accomplished" for America's first residents, while looking ahead with guarded optimism.[2]

As the first major revision of Indian regulations since 1802,[3] the act of 1834 dealt with much more than reservation boundaries. Termed a notable example of the "continuity in American Indian policy" by a comprehensive study of that policy covering most of the early national period,[4] the act in its final form contained thirty articles for the conduct of Indian-white relations, including regulations for trade and barter in Indian country, legal entry into Indian country, intruders, Indian land sales, disturbance of the peace, property indemnification and crimes in Indian country, distilleries and liquor sales to Indians, and federal judicial authority and related matters in Indian country.[5] Most of these matters have been discussed in depth elsewhere and thus—with some exceptions noted later—will not be treated here.[6]

Rather, the focus here will be on Section 1 of the 1834 act: "That all that part of the United States west of the Mississippi, and not within the states of Missouri and Louisiana, or the territory of Arkansas, and, also, that part of the United States east of the Mississippi River, and not within any state to which the Indian title has not been extinguished, for the purposes of this act, be taken and deemed to be Indian country."[7] Fifteen (50 percent) of the 1834 articles made direct reference to "Indian country"—a specific place where various regulations and prohibitions were to apply. But weak administration, chronic violations of the new Indian code, and an almost routine compression of individual reservations that culminated in a blatantly illegal white penetration of the eastern flank sector of Indian country (renamed Nebraska Territory just two decades later) suggest that the optimism of the mid-1830s was premature. At best, then, the 1834 act was urged into law as a stopgap measure for delaying non-Indian occupation of the trans-Missouri West for a decade or two. At worst, it was divisive or completely deceptive legislation from the start.

Conditions for Indians in the new Indian country continued to deteriorate in the immediate post–Civil War years and then worsened during the allotment period of the late nineteenth century. Responding to the drastic decline of the nation's Indian population by the turn of the twentieth century, non-Indian enunciations of concern for Indian well-being became commonplace and, in fact, have continued in varying degrees down to the present. Especially troubled are certain social scientists who, according to Vine Deloria, Jr., periodically forgo their academic quarters in favor of a visit to Indian country. "Every summer when school is out a veritable stream of [academic] immigrants heads into Indian country," wrote Deloria. "From every rock and cranny in the East *they* emerge, as if responding to some primeval fertility rite, and flock to reservations." These intellectual journeymen visit Indian country essentially "to make *observations*"[8] and to publish their conclusions so that others can analyze and criticize such data as a means of justifying additional and presumably no less productive intellectual excursions into Indian country.

Such less than complimentary appraisal of an academic endeavor of considerable moment might seem insensitive to the work of numerous scholars who have sincerely sought to understand Indian culture and its manifest problems since the Columbian invasion more than five centuries ago. Even so, Deloria's objection to a non-Indian presence—including that of scholars trained in the science of man—in places Indians deem their own should not be ignored, certainly not in a study that seeks to rethink the rise and fall of Indian country as provided by the 1834 law. In the Delorian genre also, but dealing with economic as opposed to intellectual exploitation in Indian country, another Indian scholar, Donald L. Fixico, has identified new villains: He charges that a combination of federal agencies, state programs, and tribal factionalism has convoluted "the original concept of Indian Country" and has thus threatened the welfare of the Indian residents there.[9]

Whether Fixico's "original concept of Indian country" harks back to Section 1 of the 1834 act is unclear, for certainly there were references to Indian country in treaties, statutes, and public pronouncements prior to that date. In fact a major obstacle to any informative and reasonably precise description of Indian country was the wide array of topographical descriptions written into treaties prior to 1834, which made it difficult, if not impossible, to determine its dimensions at any given time. That was a problem of considerable importance for federal officials then committed to the removal of thousands of eastern Indians into the region west of Missouri and Arkansas Territory.[10]

Regardless of the details of the government's plan for Indian improvement in the 1830s, at minimum it was deemed essential to determine *where* that improvement would take place. As James P. Ronda has suggested, the vast expanse of Thomas Jefferson's Louisiana Purchase of 1803, which became Jackson's equally grandiose Indian country three decades later, "was bait, a certain solution to the frontier troubles of the new republic." But in 1834 the outcome for those who would control it was anything but certain. On paper it may have appeared as an explicit geopolitical region with exterior boundaries only the most ill-informed Americans could fail to comprehend. But at another level, that of explorers, politicians, white farmers, speculators—and even Indians—the new Indian country was not just a region of valleys, prairies, plains, and mountains with flora and fauna to prove its worth. "Instead," said Ronda, "the place that became Indian Territory first had to be imagined and then created. Space had to become place."[11]

To accomplish this transformation, a dividing line on the model of frontier boundaries in Europe was deemed essential, that is, a continuous line that would replace the irregular boundaries written into Indian treaties dating back to the 1780s. Some of those boundaries extended "far into Indian country" where, according to a government report in 1817, "the causes of provocation to hostility with the Indian tribes are multiplied, and at the same time the means of protection and defence proportionately diminished."[12]

A notable precedent for establishing a continuous boundary segregating Indian country from non-Indian country was the Proclamation of 1763, issued by King George III on October 7, 1763, which prohibited unauthorized land sales and settlements west of the Appalachian divide and placed the Indians under control of the British military commander in America. Half a century later, in its report "Exchange of Lands with the Indians" (January 9, 1817), the Senate Committee on Public Lands alluded to the proclamation as a material guide for their deliberations, yet one that required modification for the amelioration of Indian-white difficulties. Whereas the Proclamation of 1763 simply sought to contain colonial expansion at the Appalachian ridge with no program for Indian improvement, the committee suggested that the Mississippi River as the dividing line for the exchange of lands between the races was a distinct improvement or, in its own words, "better calculated to remedy the inconvenience and remove the evils arising out of the present state of frontier settlements than any other within the power of Government."[13]

For a nexus between the "evils" of a scattered frontier population and the idea of a dividing line for the exchange of lands, it is instructive to consider President Jefferson's correspondence on the matter in the summer of 1803, soon after France agreed to the cession of Louisiana to the United States. On July 11, in a letter acknowledging with pleasure the congratulations offered by Horatio Gates regarding the recent diplomatic triumph in France, Jefferson informed Gates that if Congress responded to the acquisition with the wisdom the people had a right to expect, a twofold value of Louisiana for orderly American expansion was apparent: "the means of tempting all our Indians on the East side of the Mississippi to remove to the West, and of condensing instead of scattering our population."[14]

Did that mean that white settlement beyond the Mississippi would be prohibited? Was the anticipated line segregating Indians from whites absolute? Writing to John Dickinson one month later, Jefferson suggested that although the region encompassing about 50,000 inhabitants of lower Louisiana could be either annexed to Mississippi Territory or made into a new state, Louisiana above the thirty-first parallel should be used for the resettlement of Indians and to "shut up" white settlement "for a long time to come."[15] Two days later, however, he was more flexible on the question of white exclusion. "The best use we can make of the country," he wrote Senator John Breckenridge of Kentucky,

> will be to give establishments in it to the Indians on the East side of the Missipi [sic], in exchange for their present country, and open land offices . . . and thus make this acquisition the means of filling up the Eastern side, instead of drawing off it's [sic] population. When we shall be full on this side, we may lay off a range of States on the Western bank from the head to the mouth, & so, range after range, advancing compactly as we multiply.[16]

In short, there was room also for the white man west of the Mississippi, not immediately, but eventually, as a resolute force in the larger design of incorporating Indians as citizens of the United States.[17] In the meantime, in a draft of an amendment to counter anticipated constitutional concerns regarding Louisiana, Jefferson urged that white settlements in upper Louisiana be confined to military personnel and persons officially authorized to travel, explore, operate trade facilities, work salt springs and mines ("with the consent of the possessors"), and to government agents "for the cultivation of commerce, peace & good understanding with the Indians residing there."[18] It is worth recalling that Jefferson had insisted earlier that under no circumstances should white settlements be allowed on unceded Indian land: "The government will think itself bound," he wrote Secretary of War Henry Knox in 1791, "not only to declare to the Indians that such settlements are without the authority or protection of the United States, but to remove them also by force."[19]

Senate ratification of the Louisiana treaty on October 20, 1803, rendered moot the issue of a constitutional amendment and thus cleared the way for Meriwether Lewis and William Clark's "Corps of Discovery" to reconnoiter a region whose acreage had nearly doubled the land mass of the new nation. The extraordinary achievements of that journey stand prominently in the history of westward exploration. Not the least of those achievements was "an atmosphere of friendship and mutual trust between men and women who shared a common frontier life" during the course of the more-than-two-year journey from St. Louis (May 14, 1804) to the mouth of the Columbia (November 7, 1805), and then back to St. Louis (August 23, 1806).[20] From a diplomatic perspective the mission was no smashing success, for permanent tribal alliances or intertribal peace agreements eluded Lewis and Clark. But the topographical, environmental, and ethnographical data presented to government officials and then to the public provided valuable knowledge for the future relocation of Indians and, of course, the creation of a specific boundary line separating Indians from whites.

White America's population increase (exceeding 30 percent per decade between 1800 and 1850) and more particularly the dramatic economic growth consequent to the agrarian invasion of the trans-Appalachian West following the War of 1812 were the bedrock developments leading to the triumph of tribal removal and cultural segregation. Building on the Jeffersonian vision and urged on by a seemingly endless supply of sparsely occupied terrain beyond the Mississippi, the government's unwavering progression toward a new and unambiguous definition of Indian country is a familiar one to most students of federal Indian policy, namely, the forthright "Exchange of Lands Report" of the Senate Committee on Public Lands, submitted January 7, 1817, in response to a Senate resolution calling for an investigation "into the expediency of authorizing by law, an exchange of territory with any of the Indian tribes";[21] President James Monroe's assertion, also in 1817, that "the earth was given to mankind to support the greatest number of which it is capable" and his more direct call for removal of the Indians eight years later on grounds that "in their present state it is impossible to incorporate them [the Indians], in any form whatever, into our system"; President Jackson's request to Congress for "setting apart an ample district west of the Mississippi, and without the limits of any State or Territory now formed, to be guaranteed to the Indian tribes as long as they shall occupy it";[22] and the Indian Removal Act of May 28, 1830.[23]

The Indian Removal Act of 1830 invites more than casual scrutiny. The bottom line was an appropriation of $500,000 for the "exchange" of Indian lands "within the limits of any states or territories" for "any territory belonging to the United States, west of the river Mississippi, not included in any state or organized territory, and to which the Indian title has been extinguished." Nowhere in the act was the use of force required or even implied; to the contrary, it simply provided "for the reception of such tribes or nations as may *choose* [emphasis added] to exchange the lands where they now reside." No less important, certainly for the integrity of the 1834 boundary, the United States agreed to *"forever secure and guaranty* [emphasis added] to them and their heirs or successors, the country so exchanged with them."[24]

Two decades later, the "forever secure and guaranty" clause crumbled under the legislative hammer in Congress. On March 3, 1853, an ominous provision was attached to otherwise routine legislation for funding the Indian Department for the year ending June 30, 1854. It authorized the president "to enter into negotiations with the Indian tribes west of the states of Missouri and Iowa for the purpose of securing the assent of said tribes to the settlement of the citizens of the United States upon the lands claimed by said Indians, and for the purpose of extinguishing the title of said Indian tribes in whole or in part for said land."[25] Appropriated for this was $50,000, 10 percent of the amount provided for the removal program in 1830.[26] But this sum could be augmented by additional appropriations, as eventually was the case.

Whereas about 10,000 emigrant Indians, mainly from the Old Northwest (the area east of the Mississippi and northwest of the Ohio rivers), made their homes in Indian country west of Missouri in 1854, not many more than 1,000 remained in Kansas (admitted to statehood in 1861) two decades later.[27] Prospects for the Indians of nearby Nebraska (admitted in 1867), also carved out of Indian country, were no better. Calling into question the permanence of Indian land titles west of the Mississippi in general and among the Omahas, Pawnees, and Poncas of his state in particular, Nebraska Governor Robert Furnas in the early 1870s demanded that the "valuable land now held by these aborigines should be permitted to pass into the hands of intelligent, enterprising [white] citizens, who would render them productive."[28]

The governor's words proved prophetic; within a few years the circumstance of Indians in Nebraska was no better than in Kansas, prompting certain obvious questions. What had gone wrong? How was it that prior to 1873 the Pawnee, Potawatomi, Miami, Osage, Ottawa, Ponca, Kickapoo, Otoe, Delaware, Shawnee, Sac and Fox, Kansa, and Missouria people were forced to move once again, this time to much-reduced tracts in the southern part of Indian country awarded to the Five Civilized Tribes (Cherokees, Choctaws, Chickasaws, Seminoles, and Creeks) by the national government half a century earlier? Why would a Potawatomi chief, in a letter dictated through his agent to President Andrew Jackson in 1835, actually plead for a new home in Indian country even though he and his people preferred to stay in the Platte country of northwest Missouri outside the boundaries of Indian country?

To the Potawatomi leader the new boundary segregating Indians from whites seemed to offer a new chance. "This will be like a strong fence. My Father," insisted Chief Quish-Queh-Leh, "we desire to be enclosed within the strong fence, and not left on the outside." Was Quish-Queh-Leh right about the promised security of Indian country, or was his request an example of Indian naïveté regarding the true character of Indian country in the new West? Other tribal leaders were more guarded regarding the protective power of the white man's fence. After the enactment of an especially contentious treaty that forced the Winnebago people to move west of the Mississippi in 1832, Chief Whirling Thunder asserted: "I have taken my foot off your land [and] I will not put it down there again. . . . We are not like the white men. . . . This is all I have to say."[29]

A decade later the Potawatomis were still negotiating for a secure, "fenced" reservation, hopeful that it would be near the eastern border of Indian country. Federal officials in Washington, however, were determined to place them in the upper Neosho Valley, near Council Grove, in close proximity to the hostile Osages, Kansas, and

Pawnees, about 100 miles west of Missouri. With the assistance of their former subagent at Council Bluffs, the Potawatomi delegation chose their words of objection with care:

> The country is a desert prairie. It has no timber; no sugar; no fish; no game: and in many parts no water. We could not get meat, no skins, no furs, no food in that country. It has been called by the white man "the Prairie Wilderness." At Council Grove the Santa Fe traders make their last fire. Beyond this, all is prairie, nothing else.
>
> If it is such a good country that you offer why does not our *Great Father send his White children there?*[30]

But white men eventually came to understand that the "Prairie Wilderness" was no wilderness at all. Indeed, Indian country was so attractive that, based on a personal tour of Indian country in the summer of 1853, Indian Commissioner George W. Manypenny was pleased to report:

> Already the white population is occupying the lands between and adjacent to the Indian reservations, and even going west of and beyond them, and at no distant day, all the country imme-diately west of the reserves which is worth occupying, will have been taken up. . . . What a spectacle for the view of the states-man, philanthropist, Christian! With reservations dotting the eastern portion of the territory, there they stand, the represen-tatives and remnants of tribes once as powerful and dreaded, as they are now weak and dispirited.[31]

The head of the Office of Indian Affairs could thus lament the partitioning of Indian land for white benefit in future Kansas and Nebraska and even recommend (with no success) legislation to guarantee the integrity of the Indian country reservations,[32] but when all was said and done, the white advance beyond the Missouri was simply too much for a few thousand Indians located on the supposedly safe side of the fence. "In this secluded home," wrote Manypenny in 1880,

> it was believed that the efforts of the government and the philanthropist to civilize the red man, would be more successful than ever before. Such, however, was not the case. Our population advanced rapidly to the line which was to be the barrier, and with the emigration consequent upon our acquisitions from Mexico, and the organization of new territories, necessarily subjected the Indian to that kind of contact with the whites, which was sure to entail on them the vices, while deprived of the good influences of civilization.[33]

Manypenny's analysis presaged more recent studies of the problem. One published in the early 1960s concluded: "The expanse of the frontier and the multitudes of oncoming settlers were the basis of the problem. Neither the one nor the other had been adequately faced."[34] Another, focusing on the Indian Removal Act of 1830 but by implication referring to Indian country in general, pointed to related variations of the white expansion theme: greed, the transcontinental railroad, and the Kansas-Nebraska Act;[35] while still another, a monograph dealing with the demise of the "barrier philosophy" and the beginnings of the reservation system, suggested that

> from all corners came the same general advice: the tribes had to be gathered at places where they would be out of the path of white expansion and where they could be kept from harming either whites or each other. Both the friends of the Indians and those who only wanted what he possessed favored this solu-

tion. . . . The concentration of all tribes on reservations . . .
simply fulfilled by force a relatively passive policy that had
been decided upon as a response to the end of the barrier philosophy and the national expansion of the 1840's.[36]

Whatever the inherent shortcomings of the government's segregation program west of the fence, conventional wisdom has it that
Indian country as conceived in 1834 essentially fell victim to the
ubiquitous white farmer and land speculator whose desires for Indian land were intensified by the massive national land acquisitions
in Oregon and the continental southwest during the mid-1840s.
Like an Ottoman horde advancing beyond the Bosporus, nothing, it
seemed, could stop the venturesome capitalist or the man with the
plow—certainly not an imaginary line devised by Congress and
made part of permanent treaties.

"In spite of the President, and Cabinet, and Treaties," reported a
traveler from the Delaware reservation on the eastern flank of Indian country in the fall of 1854, "twelve hundred and more [white]
'sovereigns' have already, it is said, set up their thrones on these Delaware lands; and how they are to be despoiled of their kingdoms, is a
question which the Government will not readily solve."[37] Likewise, a
government surveyor on the Shawnee lands just south of the
Delawares informed Commissioner Manypenny a year later, "There
seems to be a perfect mania for acquiring lands, not only among
whites but among Indian chiefs and headmen as well."[38]

If the Potawatomis, Delawares, or Shawnees were frustrated and
uncertain over what was happening to the "strong fence," a non-
Indian observer appeared to take matters more in stride. A writer for
the *New York Tribune* maintained, "It required no spirit of divination
to foresee that, in opening the [Indian] territory to a white population, the semibarbarous occupancy of the finest lands by the Indians
would inevitably terminate in some manner."[39] But a correspondent

in the nation's capital was less certain. To understand what was happening, he wrote, "was about as easy as it would have been to unravel the knot of the Phrygian or the riddle of the Sphinx; so we very early gave up the study in despair. All that we could discern with any distinctness was the presence of unreasonable passions, selfish party aims, and unnatural prejudice."[40]

But Indian country survived, as it does to this day—remote, romantic, economically depressed, and, more often than not, a mystical entity to outsiders and generally unrecognizable by the norms of Congress in 1834. Was this "white invention" that had become a "full-blown geographic and political reality" by the end of the 1830s so pliant that its survival was virtually guaranteed,[41] even in the face of crushing national expansion and state-making in the trans-Missouri West? Had Congress simply created a temporary Indian country in 1834, a place that under federal law was fair game for Indians and non-Indians alike? A land for any and all?

Speaking for the majority of the Supreme Court, which in 1877 declared that the seizure of whiskey by federal officials in former Indian country, near the North Pacific Railroad crossing on the James River in Dakota Territory, was not a violation of a federal law that prohibited the sale or contemplated sale of alcohol in Indian country, Justice Samuel Freeman Miller summarized and commented briefly on the principal points of the ruling.[42] He noted that over the years a variety of laws regarding the actions of both Indians and non-Indians in Indian country had been passed, thus providing the essential sociopolitical, diplomatic, and geographical characteristics of Indian country in the making. Prior to 1834, continued Miller, Congress had not engaged in a serious attempt to determine "what [or where] Indian country was" for all tribes at any given time. Then, following a summary of certain legislation regarding trade and intercourse with Indians dating back to 1802, as well as related high court decisions prior to 1877, Justice Miller provided for the first time ever a comprehensive and unambiguous definition of Indian country, namely, that "the country described by the act of 1834 as Indian country remains Indian country so long as the Indians retain their original title to the soil, and ceases to be Indian country whenever they lose that title, in the absence of any different provision by treaty or by act of Congress."[43]

This seemed clear enough, even to nonjudges and nonlawyers. But what followed surely was not. In wording bordering on speculation, wording that provided considerable comfort for the architects of new territories, states, and white homesteads in Indian country, Justice Miller also held that "the Congress of the United States and the judges who administered those laws, must have found in the definition of Indian country, in the act of 1834, such an adaptability to the altered circumstances of what was then Indian country as to enable them to ascertain what it was at any time since then."[44]

Looking backward through the eyes of hundreds of white farmers comfortably situated on the prairie-plains of former Indian country in 1870, one might reasonably inquire: was Indian country west of Arkansas, Missouri, and Iowa an "altered circumstance" of the white man's vision of Indian country in 1834? The problem for Justice Miller in 1877 was the illegal sale of alcohol to Indians, but the underlying issue was precisely *where* the action took place. In the absence of Indian title to the place (clearly a part of Indian country in 1834) of the alleged illegal action, that action was not illegal, said Miller, because "the *locus in quo* was not Indian Country."[45] Did this "altered circumstance" in Dakota Territory point to the "adaptability" of Indian country in general, as Congress may have envisioned it from the start?

Looking backward also, not from pastoral farmsteads in Kansas and Nebraska or from the highest bench in the land, but from the halls of Congress, where in the decade of the 1840s the future of Indians in Indian country was becoming inextricably involved with the slavery question in the trans-Missouri West,[46] former president John

Quincy Adams shocked his fellow solons in 1841 by refusing to accept the chairmanship of the House Committee on Indian Affairs. Confiding in his diary that his acceptance of the appointment "would be a perpetual harrow upon my feelings, with a total impotence to render any useful service," he appended a devastating critique of U.S. Indian policy: "It is among the heinous sins of this nation, for which I believe God will one day bring them to judgment—but at his own time and by his own means. I turned my eyes away from the sickening mass of putrefaction."[47]

This position was a dramatic turnabout for Adams, who had supported the Puritan invasion of Algonkian New England as well as Andrew Jackson's brutal treatment of the Seminoles in Spanish Florida. Adams did not oppose the Indian Removal Act of 1830 and following his election to Congress soon thereafter he refused to support a western Indian territory that could have blocked or at least severely compromised the white advance into Indian country.[48]

His southern (as well as several northern) critics castigated him for his inconsistency, pointing out that he had disallowed an Indian presence in the "woods and templed hills that remained his ideal of America," while turning his shoulder against the agrarian democracy of the Jacksonians who had embarrassed him in 1824. But as the intellectually caustic New Englander saw it, the plantation operator who dealt in human chattel "was no better than the savage; in fact worse, for all knew the Indian loved the land for its own sake, and for profit in the marketplace." Thus for Adams to preside over the House Committee on Indian Affairs would be tantamount to his claiming that the "strong fence" policy of 1834 had been sound and workable public policy, when in fact it clearly had not. Consistency aside, as Lynn Hudson Parsons has so succinctly suggested, for Adams it was "better to let the Indian remain, than to allow the once-free lands to be tilled by the slave, or to fall under the land speculator's auction hammer."[49]

2

Reconnaissance

A ccording to the late Bernard DeVoto, celebrated litterateur and historian of the American West, 1846 was America's "Year of Decision." That was the year, we are told, when certain "manifold possibilities of chance were shaped to converge on the inevitable . . . by the actions of . . . the unremarkable commoners of the young democracy"; and it was certainly a time to rejoice for the numerous champions of Manifest Destiny. Then, when the smoke of battle had finally subsided in the fall of 1848 and the drama in Oregon, California, and the desert Southwest had run its course, DeVoto's apprehensive but still "unremarkable commoners" resumed their self-ordained tasks of breaking sod, planting grain, placing turnips and cabbages where majestic trees had once stood, promoting railroads and town sites, damming small brooks and turbulent streams, grazing cattle for slaughter and consumption in distant cities, rushing about in quest of precious metal, encroaching on Indian land in the manner of the forebears, and, of course, granting thanks to Almighty God for safe passage to the promised land.[1]

True, said DeVoto, the origins of that decisive year could be traced back "as far as one might care to go" and not a few of the consequences were "with us still."[2] But the grandiose accomplishments of these genuine Americans were at least as important as Washington's crossing of the Delaware or Jackson's defeat of the British at New Orleans in 1815. Indeed, it was high time the "Year of Decision" received its proper historical due.

In Indian country, however, that immense interior province stretching north from Texas more than 900 miles to British North America and west from the Mississippi River (excluding the states of Louisiana, Arkansas, and Missouri) more than 700 miles to the snowy peaks of the Continental Divide, the year 1846 was decisive as well. Some of its native residents had inhabited the eastern border of Indian country since the late seventeenth century, whereas others had been forcibly "removed" there by the federal government beginning in the mid-1820s—ostensibly for economic and cultural improvement but in fact for not much more than physical survival. Still others, in greater numbers and principally from the Great Lakes region, the lower Ohio Valley, and the slave-holding South, had been driven to new and unfamiliar terrain in Indian country in the 1830s and 1840s, to locations dangerously close to the so-called Great American Desert.[3] Collectively, in 1846 these first Americans were at an historical juncture no less significant than that faced by DeVoto's "unremarkable commoners" in the West that same year.

A necessary prelude to the application of DeVoto's analysis to the increasingly alarming conditions in Indian country in 1846 is the consideration of a treaty negotiated in 1825 by St. Louis Indian Superintendent William Clark with the Kansa (or Kaw) tribe, a Dhegiha-Siouan people inhabiting the area north and west of present-day Kansas City since at least the mid-seventeenth century. The treaty provided legal recognition of the tribe's ownership and occupancy rights to the northern half of the present state of Kansas and all the area south of the Great Nemaha River in present-day Nebraska. But however generous this ownership may have been perceived at the time by the Kansa people, it was temporal and wholly illusory. In fact, Clark's main objective, clearly stated in Articles 1 and 2 of the 1825 treaty, was to reduce the tribe's traditional land holdings by more than 20,000,000 acres, to a strip of land beginning near present-day Topeka and extending as far west as the president of the United States in the future might deem necessary—and as eventually determined, to the 102nd meridian and comprising more than 5,750,000 acres.[4] Thus by the simple sweep of the treaty pen, a massive domain was legally cleared for the relocation of thousands of "emigrant," or "removal," Indians, whose transfer under federal supervision to a distant and remote place called Indian country would be largely completed by 1846.

Nevertheless, the reduction of Indian land in Indian country continued unabated. In 1846 the Kansa domain was diminished even more drastically, this time to a 20-mile-square reservation near Council Grove, a Santa Fe Trail landmark in the Neosho Valley 100 miles west of the Missouri state line.[5] In the same year, disparate clans and bands of Potawatomi, Chippewa, and Ottawa people, whom government dignitaries arbitrarily proclaimed "The Potawatomi Nation," were induced to relinquish an additional 8,000,000 acres, bringing the total of Indian country lands ceded to more than 10,000,000 by 1846.[6] In the absence of evidence that the government was in need of such vast acreage for still more Indians, what were the reasons for these additional cessions? For benefit of the recently arrived removal tribes or, perhaps, for the earlier resident Osages, Kansas, or Pawnees? For a buffer zone between the planter tribes from the east and the more nomadic and often more belligerent hunter tribes to the west? For railroad and town development? To put in place an obstacle to the expansion of slavery west of Missouri? To reward DeVoto's white "commoners" with more land to plow? To demonstrate once and for all that Indian country—ceded or otherwise—was attractive, indeed destined, for non-Indian settlement?

Edwin Bryant, prominent coeditor of the *Louisville Courier* and outspoken critic of the Jackson administration and its Indian policy, was clearly sympathetic to the latter possibility. On May 5, 1846, less than a month after the second Kansa land cession treaty had been ratified, Bryant embarked for California from Independence, Missouri, a few miles from the eastern border of Indian country. By May 24 his wagon train had arrived at the Vermillion Creek crossing of the Oregon-California Trail. In this setting, not unlike the much broader Kansas River valley only a few miles to the south, his appraisal was one of distinct admiration and certainly of considerable interest to overland emigrants accustomed to repeated accounts of the aridity and infertility of Indian country. Wrote Bryant:

> The banks above and below the ford are well supplied with oak, elm, and linden trees of good size, and the land, which on the western side rises from the creek in gentle undulations, is of the richest composition, and covered with a carpet of the greenest and most luxuriant vegetation. We found here, gushing from a ledge of limestone rock, a spring of excellent water. . . . Rising from the bottom of this stream, upon the tableland, the scenery for a long distance to the north and the south is surpassingly attractive. . . .
>
> It is impossible to travel through this [Indian] country with the utilitarian eye and appreciation natural to all Americans, without a sensation of regret that an agricultural resource of such immense capacity as is here supplied by a bountiful providence, is so utterly neglected and wasted.
>
> The soil, I am persuaded, is capable of producing every variety of crop adapted to this latitude, which enters into the consumption and conduces to the comfort and luxury of man, with a generosity or reproduction that would appear almost

marvelous to the farmers of many of our agricultural districts on the coast of the Atlantic.[7]

A week later, Bryant, who was by then on the banks of the Big Blue River near the present Kansas-Nebraska line, continued to praise the agricultural potential of Indian country. Conceding an occasional "sparseness of timber," he nevertheless declared the region "the most desirable, in an agricultural point of view, of any which I have ever seen. It possesses such natural wealth and beauties, that at some future day it will be the Eden of America."[8]

Other travelers confirmed, albeit in less biblical terms, the alluring character of Indian country. Such was the notice of Heinrich Lienhard, a Swiss excursionist en route from New Orleans to Sutter's Fort in California. While passing across the Shawnee and Delaware reservations 50 miles west of Fort Leavenworth in 1846, Lienhard was enthralled with the "undulating, rich prairie" and the "gratifying" panorama stretching out before him, made all the more pleasing "by a running stream, discernible from afar by a growth of trees along its banks." In fact, to reassure those who feared deprivation and possible suffering in Indian country, Lienhard insisted that he and his companions "had no reason to complain about any lack of grass, water, firewood. . . . [F]or our purposes," reported Lienhard, "we found plenty everywhere."[9] And in response to a report that a party of Oregon emigrants had lost their way in the same area that Bryant and Lienhard had traversed only a year earlier, the editor of a St. Joseph, Missouri, newspaper indicated no special concern for their well-being. Rather, he matter-of-factly suggested that they probably were "out planting buckwheat so as to have sufficient provisions when they continued their journey the following spring." In fact, the *Gazette* offered, "The emigrants might well decide to settle permanently in their new location."[10]

The *Gazette* understood, of course, that non-Indian settlement in Indian country was then illegal. Nevertheless, by the mid-1840s the prospect of white settlement west of Missouri and Iowa had become by no means idle speculation. "This country is so beautifully adapted to cultivation that there is driven from the mind all idea of it being a wild waste in the wilderness," wrote a Mormon emigrant about the Platte Valley 80 miles west of present-day Omaha in the spring of 1847, at a time when Mormon leaders were still considering future Nebraska as a desirable location for their permanent settlements. "The fields in the woods and the habitations of men are what one is continually looking for," was his wistful lament.[11] Two months later, another Mormon emigrant called the area near Grand Island, several days' travel farther west, "as fine a country ever I saw for farming or grazing."[12] And still another emigrant, this one a young woman traveling west in search of a new life in Utah, pensively described the flowers and other vegetation at Ash Fork near the eastern Wyoming line, in the summer of 1850, "as delicate and interesting looking as if they were raised in well cultivated gardens in the East."[13]

Certainly there were numerous non-Indian observers of Indian country during the decade of the 1840s. According to one account, 1,350 people traveled across the central prairie-plains to Oregon or California by way of the Kansas and Big Blue valleys in 1846.[14] The total overland travel that same year, according to another count, was 2,700. By 1847 the number had increased to 4,450, and after the discovery of California gold in 1848, more than 25,000 Argonauts crossed Indian country in the great rush of 1849.[15] Certainly the push of continental expansion in the 1840s placed the national government in the role of calling public attention—inadvertently, for the most part—to the topographical and climatic characteristics of Indian country. Three months after the declaration of war against Mexico (May 13, 1846), 1,500 mounted volunteers and several companies of the First Dragoons, together totaling about 1,700 men, marched over the Santa Fe Trail from Fort Leavenworth to Santa Fe under the command of Colonel Stephen Watts Kearny.[16] By mid-century the number of military personnel or persons under some sort of federal assignment or employment who had traveled this overland route through the very heart of Indian country had increased by the thousands. In addition, there were scores of private commercial expeditions, for example, the twenty-two wagons of Bent, St. Vrain & Co. that left Bent's Fort in mid-May 1846 and arrived in Missouri a month later.[17]

Thus a veritable drove of potential white settlers traversed Indian country in the 1840s. In what surely would be the envy of a modern real estate broker, the promotional impact of this great migration can hardly be overstated, and for the thousands of Indians who only recently had been forced to establish new homes in the unfamiliar environment of Indian country, the future was anything but secure. And such insecurity was not lessened after the passage, on May 13, 1846, of a bill to construct a chain of military fortifications along the Oregon Trail.

Under pressure to improve the Indian service without diminishing or presenting an obstacle to national expansion as implied by the military fortification bill, Indian Commissioner William Medill dispatched circulars to his field superintendents on how best to deal with those tribes with little experience with federal authority or those in the direct path of expansion. Among the more reasoned responses to the circular was that of Thomas H. Harvey, head of the St. Louis Superintendency, whose jurisdiction included most of Indian country under the 1834 law. Included in Superintendent Harvey's critical response to what he viewed as the accelerating and seemingly unregulated white advance into the region west of Missouri and Iowa was his recommendation that because of the "*interest of the Whites upon the prairies*" (emphasis added), it was mandatory that the government place "efficient" federal officials in Indian country, officials clearly capable of dealing with the invasion of Indian country.[18] Indeed, the situation had become so dangerous by 1846 that some federal officials considered removing the Indians once again, this time far distant from the paths of the white advance west of Missouri and Iowa. This idea of a secondary removal, according to a thorough and widely cited study of federal Indian policy in the mid-1840s, "had been brewing for some time."[19]

Arguments regarding the full reach of the "Great American Desert" in Indian country as defined by the 1834 law had also been brewing. Prior to the celebrated (and controversial) reports of Zebulon M. Pike (1810) and Stephen H. Long (1823), which, taken together, placed the heart of the "desert" somewhere between the 100th and 101st meridians north of the Arkansas River in present-day west-central Kansas,[20] a variety of early–nineteenth century accounts firmly disputed the extension of the "desert" into eastern and even east-central Kansas and Nebraska. The same could be said for the area as far north as central North Dakota, according to the government explorer Meriwether Lewis. In a letter to his mother from Fort Mandan near present-day Bismarck in the spring of 1805, Lewis observed that by previous "intelligence" he had been warned that the country above the mouth of the Platte would be "barren, sterile and sandy"—good evidence of a desert environment. But based on personal observation, that certainly was not the case. In fact, wrote the co-leader of President Jefferson's Corps of Discovery, the topography at Fort Mandan and the nearby Mandan villages was

> fertile in the extreme, the soil being from one to twenty feet in depth, consisting of a fine loam, intertwined with a sufficient quantity of sand only to induce a luxuriant growth of grass and other vegetable productions. . . . It is also generally level, yet well watered; in short there can be no objection to it except

that of a want of timber . . . [which] is by no means attributable to a deficiency in the soil to produce it, but owes its origin to the ravages of fires, which the natives kindle in the plains at all seasons of the year.[21]

Five hundred miles south of the encampment where Lewis composed the letter to his mother in 1805, the French-Canadian merchant Charles Le Raye recorded in his journal on October 29, 1801, that the Kansas River west of the present Kansas City was "a handsome stream" flowing through "a rolling and rich country." The area to the north was no less appealing. Veering north at a point just west of present-day Topeka, Le Raye described the lower Platte country as "rich and level, with wood near the water."[22] Indeed, like Lewis and others who would follow in their footsteps, Le Raye's esteem for the trans-Missouri West belied the complaint, even from abroad, that a lack of reliable information or just plain ignorance led to the government's selection of an arid wasteland where the remnants of America's first human inhabitants might be expected to survive.

From across the Atlantic in London came unrestrained criticism of the Americans' apparent geographical ignorance, certainly by comparison to the English. The English, explained the *Eclectic Review* in 1811, would never rest satisfied until even the slightest expanse of countryside was "raised into renown by a costly topographical quarto, or even, if it is a particularly ambitious lot of acres, by the whole graphical and typographical honours of an imperial folio." But His Majesty's former subjects in America, by contrast, seemed blissfully content to remain topographically ignorant, indeed, to leave hundreds of thousands of square miles wholly unknown, "without an adventure of research, a measurement, a map, a Flora, or a set of views; leaving them with . . . hardly the distinction of a name, to display the various aspects of climates, and the changing of seasons. . . . If they are occasionally moved . . . to send a deputation of eyes across a few parallels of the hemisphere, it is marvelous to find how little shall at last be brought back."[23]

Even so, the circumscribed but informative Patrick Gass account of the Lewis and Clark expedition to the Pacific, in conjunction with the more-detailed reports of Major Pike's trek across Louisiana to the Rocky Mountains in search of the sources of the Arkansas and Red rivers, prompted speculation that a new trend in climatic and topographical discernment in the trans-Missouri West might be in the offing, what the *Review* called a "hopeful beginning" and an important development that might pave the way for integrating scientific data with America's emerging national purpose.[24] And in a more recent view, the *Review*'s analysis and that of Gass foreshadowed the work of William H. Goetzmann, who in 1966 convincingly marked nineteenth-century American exploration beyond the Missouri as a purposeful undertaking in which the national government played a prominent role. In passages particularly relevant to understanding the impermanent character of Indian country under the 1834 law, Goetzmann emphasized that the "process" was "emulative," that is, a modus operandi, with settlers following the lead of the explorers (both public and private) whose expeditions and reports mirrored "national images and plans."[25]

Contrary to the gloomy desert accounts of Pike and Long were the climatic data reported by John Bradbury, commissioned by the Botanical Society of Liverpool to investigate plant life in the western United States. Bradbury was invited to Monticello and on Jefferson's advice selected St. Louis as the base for his scientific operations. There, in early 1811, he met Wilson Price Hunt, commander of John Jacob Astor's Pacific expedition. Hunt invited Bradbury to accompany his party to the Arikara villages by way of the Missouri River and what is now north-central South Dakota. In his *Travels in the Interior of America*, published in Liverpool in 1817 and widely read in

America, Bradbury noted that "amongst intelligent Americans the question of whether it [the prairie-plains of future Indian country] can or cannot be peopled by civilized man? has often been agitated. . . . [A]ccustomed as they are to a profusion of timber for buildings, fuels, and fence," continued Bradbury, the Americans had concluded that the absence of such "commodities" meant that much of the region west of the Missouri River could not be cultivated. But with the need for only a small amount timber for the construction of fences and buildings and the profusion of coal on the prairies and deposits of salt, clay, and gypsum in ample supply in the lower Arkansas Valley, the Americans were simply misguided. "My own opinion," wrote Bradbury, "is that it can be cultivated, and that, in process of time, it will not only be peopled and cultivated, but that it will be one of the most beautiful countries of the world."[26]

On this point Henry Marie Brackenridge was less optimistic. Based on "contemporary" reports and his own observations while traveling with Manual Lisa up the Missouri River to the Mandan villages in 1811, the American traveler and geographer described the first 200 miles west of the Mississippi (roughly the present Missouri-Kansas border) as "well-timbered" and the soil "generally good." But for the next 300 miles, to approximately the 100th meridian, the country could "scarcely be said to admit of settlements." In fact, the "prevailing idea" that the vast expanse beyond the Missouri was susceptible of cultivation and thus capable of sustaining a permanent population was simply "erroneous." Still, Brackenridge qualified his assessment by noting that the river bottoms draining the country due west of the Missouri, "being generally fine and in many spots truly beautiful," could in fact "bear cultivation." Indeed, in what turned out as solid prophecy regarding Indian country in the future, Brackenridge cautioned that "did not the Indians possess it, there would in a very short time, be many small groups of [white] settlements scattered through it."[27]

Brackenridge was a private excursionist who gathered data and then published his findings for the public in general, with no specific agenda regarding Indians and their future in either the East or the West. U.S. Indian Factor George C. Sibley, in contrast, was directly involved in Indian affairs (and policy enforcement) and presumably as trustworthy as Brackenridge—if not more so—on the subject of how habitable the western prairie-plains actually were. A former assistant factor at Fort Bellefontaine near St. Louis, Sibley was the first head factor at the Fort Osage Factory, established in 1808 on a bluff overlooking the Missouri River 40 miles below the mouth of the Kansas River. The site for this government Indian factory (or trade center) had been selected by Indian Agent William Clark and intended as a combination military fortification and trade station to police intertribal relations and to provide a dependable supply of trade goods at fair prices for the Osage, Kansa, Ioway, and Otoe-Missouria tribes in that area. And as the federal facility then closest to future Indian country, it served as Sibley's point of departure for his expedition to the West in the spring of 1811.[28]

The objectives of the expedition were several and had apparently been worked out in consultation with Agent Clark in St. Louis. Clark and Sibley sought to mend relations between the warring Kansas and Pawnees and to forge more cordial relations with these and the other tribes in the region. With a second war with Britain on the horizon, there was also concern over the possibility of British and Spanish military alliances with the Kansas and Pawnees, and perhaps the Osages as well. A trader who had only recently arrived from the Pawnee villages, for example, advised Sibley that 600 Spaniards—more than twice the number estimated by Lieutenant Pike—were planning a military campaign to the Loup-Platte country and the construction of a military installation near the Pawnees. From a different perspective, the expansionist-minded Sibley viewed the threatened war with Britain as a logical opportunity for the

United States to take control of at least some of the Spanish South-west. There were no announced scientific objectives of the expedition, but since Sibley was an inquisitive individual with a keen "scientific curiosity" as well as an energetic explorer who informed his superiors of his intent to personally visit the renowned Grand Saline on the Salt Fork of the Arkansas 300 miles southwest of Fort Osage, his observations were obviously of more than casual interest to Clark, to whom he reported at the conclusion of his journey.[29]

Sibley left Fort Osage on May 11, 1811, and returned two months later. He traveled several days with an Osage hunting party en route to the western bison country and spent several days at the main Kansa village near the confluence of the Big Blue and Kansas rivers. On May 23, in company with nine Osages and seven Kansas, he headed north along a line midway between the ninety-eighth and ninety-ninth meridians to a large Pawnee village on the Loup River 30 miles west of present-day Columbus, Nebraska. From there he moved 200 miles south to a Little Osage hunting camp near what is now Hutchinson, Kansas, and from there he traveled southwest to the Grand Saline ("280 miles southwest of Fort Osage") in the present Alfalfa County, Oklahoma, and then to the rugged "Rock Saline" area near the 100th meridian in present-day Harper County, Oklahoma. His return trip took him through southern Kansas and then northeast along the Osage tract back to Fort Osage, which he reached on July 11, 1811. He had traversed more than 1,000 miles of future Indian country, and for the segment of his trip from the Pawnee village to the Arkansas River, his route was only a few miles east of Pike's five years earlier.[30]

Even though Sibley introduced his report to Clark as "a brief account of my late tour to the Indian country," much of the terrain he crossed was not then claimed by Indian people, and it was not legally viewed as a formal "Indian country" by the United States or any foreign power at that time. Nor was it a gloomy, inhospitable desert. The Kansa village, reported Sibley, was located "in a charming elevated prairie of small extent . . . overlooked by a chain of lofty naked hills, which gives a romantic effect to the scene." The Kansas River there was about 100 feet wide, a gentle and possibly navigable stream that drained "a fine tract of country." The Pawnee village to the north was sensibly located "on a beautiful level prairie on the north bank of the Wolf [Loup] branch of the Platte." Heading south to the Arkansas River, which was "nearly two hundred yards wide, rapid, shallow and red," Sibley and his party crossed a verdant prairie en route to the Osage Chief White Hair's village just across the Kansas-Oklahoma border south of the present Wichita. Here, about 225 miles southwest of Fort Osage, Sibley represented the surroundings as anything but desert:

> They [White Hair's people] possess a country abounding in game, of all kinds. The buffaloe are always within two days walk of their town, and afford them ample supplies of food and winter clothing. The climate is salubrious and pleasant, the soil fertile and fruitful. The winters are moderate. It is not surprising that these people are so strongly attached to their present residence.[31]

Little wonder, then, that when William Clark—who had been promoted to head the St. Louis Indian Superintendency in 1822—was called upon to recommend an area west of Missouri for a deputation of Creek leaders to examine for possible tribal relocation under Article 4 of the Indian Springs Treaty of February 12, 1825,[32] he harked back to Sibley's report of 1811. Indeed, some of Clark's words to the War Department in 1825 had a familiar ring:

> I find, from information derived from persons to be relied upon, that the country embraced in these cessions [from the

Kansa and Osage tribes in 1825] is wonderfully adapted to an Indian population. . . . Grass is universally abundant, and the winters, in a great portion of the cession, mild enough to winter cattle, horses, and many other domestic animals. . . . On all creeks and rivers there are bottoms of rich land, easily prepared for cultivation. The country is divided into woodland or prairie, (but mostly prairie,) and is well watered by springs and running streams, and convenient to the salt plains and springs of strong salt water, from which an inexhaustible supply of salt can be obtained; and also to the great buffalo ranges, from which supplies can be obtained until they can be supplied from their own flocks.[33]

Although such intelligence may have raised the eyebrows of those under the sway of Pike, Long, and other partisans of a bona fide desert somewhere west of the Mississippi,[34] Clark's words to the contrary had been anticipated by August Storrs in a letter to Missouri Senator Thomas Hart Benton around five months earlier. Storrs, a prominent resident of Franklin, Missouri, and veteran Santa Fe Trail traveler, waxed eloquent on the wonderful country west of Missouri, a terrain ideally suited to the Indians' every need. Wrote Storrs to Benton:

Nature could hardly have formed a country more admirably fitted to such a purpose, than that which lies between us [at the western border of Missouri] and the Arkansas river. It is among the most beautiful and fertile tracts of country I ever saw. Streams, lined with timber, intersect and beautify it in every direction. There are delightful landscapes, over which Flora has scattered her beauties with a wanton hand, and upon whose bosom innumerable wild animals display their amazing numbers. The spring clothes this solitude with its richest scenery, and affords a combination which cannot fail to please the eye and delight the imagination. . . . As I passed through that delightful region, I could not help regretting that it should be a waste of nature, and felt a secret assurance that, at some future period, flocks would feed upon its abundant herbage, and a numerous population would derive support from its fertility.[35]

Storrs admitted to a "want of timber" in the uplands, but since it was doubtful that the emigrant tribes would be combined into compact communities on the model of white settlements east of the Mississippi, this deficiency posed no obstacle to successful Indian resettlement. Like Sibley, Storrs also called attention to the extensive salt deposits nearby and the countless buffaloes and wild horses simply there for the taking. In short, the area between Missouri and the Great Bend of the Arkansas, extending south into what is now Oklahoma and north to the Platte, was hardly a gloomy desert alien to human occupation.[36]

Such was the conclusion also of Francis Paul Prucha more recently, in an article well construed to demonstrate that the federal government never intended to "dump the Indians into the desolate wastes of the Great American Desert." In fact, stressed Prucha, whose analysis was based on a variety of government documents, maps, and atlases, none of the terrain actually parceled out to the Indians from the mid-1820s to the mid-1840s was "conceived at the time to be an inhabitable desert."[37] But if the area was habitable for Indians, was it not equally attractive to non-Indians as well? Were Bradbury, Sibley, Clark, and Storrs recounting the virtues of future Indian country for the benefit of removal Indians alone?

Certainly the critical assessment of Indian country continued *after* the Indian Removal Act went into effect on May 28, 1830. Four months after that date, Baptist missionary and government adviser—surveyor Isaac McCoy, for example, reported that the country north of the Kansas River and west of the Missouri was "better" than he had expected and that his final report would be more favorable than he had anticipated. And so it was. In company with some Delaware scouts McCoy took the survey 210 miles west of Missouri. In spite of what he called an "uncommon" drought then afflicting the area, as well as a prairie fire that roared past his party, McCoy observed numerous buffaloes, elk, and antelope. The soil was "invariably rich" and all the bottom lands of the Solomon River and smaller streams nearby were "of the first rate quality." Indeed, reported McCoy, "the country under consideration may be safely considered favorable for settlement."[38]

In the fall of 1832, from a point near present-day Stillwater, Oklahoma, about 250 miles south of the area only recently reconnoitered by McCoy, Henry L. Ellsworth confided in a letter to his wife that the public was simply uninformed regarding the beauty and fertility of the prairies west of Arkansas Territory. A member of the Stokes Commission, which had been designated by Congress to examine and report on the suitability of that area for relocating southern Indians, Ellsworth wrote that the land was "good enough" for the Indians, and that the considerable land improvements of the thousands of Creeks, Cherokees, and Choctaws already there were evidence that the area was well suited for human settlement. "The flowers of spring have disappeared," noted Ellsworth with a tinge of romantic nostalgia, "and have left numerous stalks covered with seeds as mementoes of vernal fragrance"—a description not at odds with that of his distinguished travel companion Washington Irving, who opined, "the most splendid parks in England did not surpass the beautiful scenery around us." And for the die-hard naysayers, there were the words of Dr. Thomas O'Dwyer, another member of the Ellsworth party, who insisted that "Eden was here, not on the Euphrates."[39]

In his 1832 dispatch to the War Department, this time dealing with the Cherokee and Creek surveys in the future Oklahoma and

Secretary of War John Eaton's proposed design for a strategically located intertribal tract, or "common ground on which individuals of any tribe might settle [in the west]," Isaac McCoy reminded his Indian Office superiors of the enormous acreage of Indian country then contemplated by Congress, as well as the considerable amount of land not needed by the emigrant tribes who might be relocated there. What was the best use for this surplus land? Although it could not be sold without the government's permission, McCoy was firmly convinced that "every tribe possessing more land than it wants . . . would be happy to have others settle near them." But why was this desirable? McCoy's answer was reasonable and agreeable to the basic tenets of emerging Jacksonian economic policy: "The merchant would desire to multiply his neighbors to enable him to extend his sales and the owner of a mill would be pleased with the increase in his customers."[40]

McCoy, who probably spent more time in the future Indian country than any other non-Indian prior to 1834, has been viewed as a dedicated and energetic but misguided Indian reformer, an idealist victimized by his "obsession" with Indian colonization and pan-tribalism as a means toward Indian statehood.[41] His obsessiveness notwithstanding, it is important to understand that at a formative juncture in the implementation of removal policy, McCoy took it upon himself to advise the Indian Office of an impending surplus of fertile, nonarid land west of Missouri and Arkansas, and in so doing served as a driving force leading to the 10,000,000-acre land cessions of the Kansa and Potawotomi people more than a decade later. McCoy's implied question was whether it was sound policy to throw up a "strong fence" around virgin Indian country, and thus segregate the emigrant tribes from merchants, millers, and farmers—the very people who might guide the Indians on the road to civilization.

Clearly there was pressure for white settlement west of Missouri in the years preceding the Indian Trade and Intercourse Act of 1834.

In 1820, the year prior to Missouri's statehood, Howard County, on the cutting edge of the state's agrarian frontier and located midway between present-day St. Louis and Kansas City, had a population of 12,000. At the nearby Boonslick land office, opened in 1819, land was then selling at an average of $4.00 per acre, in contrast to $2.84 at the St. Louis land office. By 1821, with a population increase to 13,427, Howard had become the most rapidly growing and most populous of the state's fifteen counties. But there was demand for still more land; it was hoped that land would become available by means of a major Sac and Fox–Ioway cession north of the Missouri River and an equally massive Osage-Kansa cession to the west.[42]

All of that did not go unnoticed by George C. Sibley at Fort Osage or by William Clark, then governor of Missouri Territory. Acting under Clark's instructions and obviously cognizant of the territorial legislature's design to move the western Missouri line 40 miles west of its location at that time, Factor Sibley invited the head chiefs and warriors of the Kansa nation to a council at Fort Osage. The Kansas had a history of obstruction to white advances west of modern-day Kansas City, at the confluence of the Missouri and Kansas rivers, so it was mandatory that Sibley offer gifts and promises of future merchandise and services to secure the land in question. Finally, on September 20, 1818, the Kansa chiefs and warriors agreed to cede land in the 40-mile district and a tract in western Missouri Territory for "one thousand dollars in suitable merchandise at fair prices" plus a comparable annual distribution or its equivalent in cash, apparently in perpetuity. In addition, the Kansas demanded the free services of a blacksmith and ongoing military protection of the United States. Sibley insisted that the merchandise and other concessions were "a mere trifle as compared with the immense value of the land," but the "agreement" came to naught, most likely because neither Clark nor Sibley had advance clearance from the Indian Office in Washington.[43]

The 40-mile district directly west of what is now Kansas City would become the most valuable segment of the entire Indian country under the act of 1834. It would also become the focus of seemingly endless disputes—legal and otherwise—in the decades to come. Sibley's words to Missouri Senator David Barton from Fort Osage, dated January 10, 1824, were at once a commentary on the failed negotiations with the Kansa Indians in 1818 and a prophecy of what was on the horizon:

> It is vain to attempt to restrain our people. . . . I believe there are more than an hundred instances within my own knowledge of men with families, who are now squatters on the public land, who are able to purchase, but who will not 'till they can purchase the tract I am speaking of. Meanwhile they are utterly useless to themselves or the state, living upon the bounties of nature, the venison and honey and wild fruits of the land. They necessarily contract habits of violence and a sort of semi-savage barbarism of manners that in some degree unfits them for the duties of civilized life. They are in short homeless wanderers— and such is the stubbornness of their nature that they will rather remain as they are than to forego the great privilege of occupying the home of their free choice.[44]

3

Preparing the Way

Writing to his Indian Office superiors in Washington from Fort Zarah in central Kansas in May 1866, Kiowa-Comanche Agent Jesse H. Leavenworth requested clarification regarding the legal boundaries of Indian country. Alcohol, under the law that had established Indian country more than three decades earlier, was an illicit trade item with Indians in Indian country, and Agent Leavenworth had ordered a liquor trader "of the name of Dietz" operating in the vicinity of Fort Zarah to leave Indian country for having supplied the Indians of his agency "with all [the alcohol] they wanted." But Dietz had brazenly ignored the order and even threatened legal action if Leavenworth did not desist.[1]

Leavenworth certainly was no novice in Indian country. A graduate of West Point and son of the distinguished General Henry Leavenworth, after whom Fort Leavenworth was named, the younger Leavenworth was instrumental in organizing the Georgetown Mining District west of Denver in 1859, and by 1861 had secured dual appointments as a U.S. deputy marshal of Colorado Territory and colonel and commander of the Second Regiment Colorado Volunteers. Two years later, on June 8, 1863, he was named "Commander of

All Troops on the Santa Fe Trail in the District of Kansas." Four months later, however, Leavenworth was abruptly dismissed from his regular army appointment on grounds of "deceptive conduct in the recruitment of the Second Colorado Volunteers" back in 1861. Convinced that military politics and especially the machinations of certain Colorado territorial officials were responsible for what he viewed as a trumped-up charge, Leavenworth took his case directly to Washington, where the judge advocate general found him guilty of no legal infraction. President Lincoln signed the finding on March 4, 1864, and was so impressed with Leavenworth's service on the Colorado frontier that he offered him a brevet brigadier general-ship. But the former Santa Fe Trail commander was fed up with the military and declined the offer in favor of an Interior Department appointment to head the newly created Kiowa-Comanche Indian Agency, which in May 1866 was temporarily headquartered at Fort Zarah.[2]

There is no doubt that Agent Leavenworth feared a suit brought by trader Dietz for having seized his supposed personal property, that is, alcohol, and for having disrupted and perhaps destroyed his business with the Kiowas and Comanches as well as his other native customers in the vicinity of Fort Zarah. With this in mind, Agent Leavenworth requested that it be *"distinctly stated"* by the commissioner of Indian Affairs whether Fort Zarah and the Santa Fe Trail—less than a quarter mile from the fort—were or were not in Indian country.[3] It was a reasonable and certainly important query, but there is no evidence that the Indian Office responded to Leavenworth's dispatch. Other matters in and around Fort Zarah, apparently, were of greater moment. For one thing, the Kiowas and Comanches were then in process of being confined to a diminished reservation hundreds of miles south of the Fort Zarah area,[4] and in the larger picture, the boundaries of Indian country dating back to the 1834 law had become increasingly blurred in the face of white homesteading, railroad construction, and town building that followed in the wake of Kansas statehood in 1861.

In fact there was uncertainty from the start regarding an Indian country exclusively for Indians in the West. In September 1834, soon after the Indian country was formalized by law, a prominent eastern newspaper heartily endorsed a proposal from the House Committee on Indian Affairs calling for the establishment of a Western Territory in Indian country that "forever" would be the exclusive domain of the Indians. The total acreage for the territory was estimated at 132,295,680 acres, to be divided as follows: 15,628,000 acres for the indigenous tribes such as the Osages, Kansas, Pawnees, and the plains tribes farther west, 46,202,000 acres for the removal, or "emigrant," tribes—enough to provide 326 acres for each Indian—and 70,465,680 acres in a more general category labeled "unappropriated."[5] In short, according to the paper's calculations, more than half of the proposed Western Territory would be available for purposes other than providing homes and subsistence for Indians, emigrant or otherwise. The Western Territory bill failed,[6] but the publicity accompanying its consideration focused national attention on an undeveloped region of the United States that had been the object of strategic and commercial interest as early as 1821.

On September 1, 1821, William Becknell and five men had left Franklin, Missouri, with their pack animals on a "trading trip" to the Comanche country that ultimately took them to Santa Fe. Their route was west from Franklin to Fort Osage, southwest to the great bend of the Arkansas River, along the Arkansas to the mouth of the Purgatory, then on to San Miguel, and finally to Santa Fe, which they reached in mid-November. By the following January, with "specie, mules, asses & Spanish blankets" as proof of their mercantile skill, Becknell and his men were back in Franklin. Becknell returned to Santa Fe in 1822, this time with wagons loaded with trade merchandise far in excess of the previous year. In subsequent years the

Santa Fe Trail commerce grew to such an extent that on March 3, 1825—responding to the economic interests of the overland traders and pressure exerted by Senator Thomas Hart Benton of Missouri, who in the Senate chamber waved a map of the government road from Georgia to New Orleans given to him by Thomas Jefferson and demanded a like favor for the "new West"—the government authorized the expenditure of $10,000 to survey and mark the road from the Missouri frontier to the international boundary, plus another $20,000 to negotiate with Indians for a right-of-way across that vast region.[7]

The survey and marking of the trail were carried out without incident in the summer of 1825 by federal commissioners George C. Sibley, Thomas Mather, and Benjamin Reeves, assisted by surveyor Joseph C. Brown and additional support personnel. Negotiations with the Osage and Kansa tribes for the right-of-way were concluded without difficulty as well. Sibley and his fellow commissioners met with the Great and Little Osage chiefs and headmen "at the place called Council Grove, on the River Nee-o-sho [Neosho], one hundred and sixty miles southwest of Fort Osage" on August 10, 1825, and for a payment of $500 "in money or merchandise, at their option" secured an agreement that both bands of Osages would allow the survey and marking to go forward and that the road so surveyed and marked would "be forever free for the use of the citizens of the United States and of the Mexican Republic, who shall at all times pass and repass without hindrance or molestation on the part of the Great and Little Osages." These agreements were entered into Articles 1 and 2 of the treaty, but Article 4 went much further by providing that the Osages "do further consent and agree that the road aforesaid shall be considered as extending to a reasonable distance on either side, so that travelers thereon may, at any time, leave the marked tract, for the purpose of finding subsistence and proper camping places." Six days later, "at Sora Kansas Creek, two hundred and thirty-eight miles southwestwardly from Fort Osage," a treaty similar in all respects was signed by certain chiefs and headmen of the Kansa tribe. Both treaties were proclaimed law on May 3, 1826.[8]

Precisely what was meant by "a reasonable distance on either side . . . of the marked tract" and "proper camping places" is not known, but even a cautiously conservative interpretation of Article 4 suggests that Santa Fe Trail travelers could move onto Osage and Kansa land wherever their search for buffalo, antelope, fowl, fish, maize, potatoes, or wild onions might lead them, and that they could remain on such land as long as they continued their search for natural subsistence. It was invitation enough to excite the novice and seasoned squatter alike, an inducement made all the more appealing by a lack of evidence in the commissioners' final report to the War Department that a "Great American Desert" awaited merchants and traders heading west toward Santa Fe. True, noted Sibley and his aides, the boundless prairie-plains west of Missouri might excite a sense of "dull and tedious monotony" for some, particularly if their journey were accentuated by the presence of a blistering sun. But a blistering sun could be experienced elsewhere in the United States, in Independence or Little Rock or on a fairly regular basis east of the Mississippi and south of the Potomac. More to the point was the existence of a spectacular timberland at Council Grove a "quarter of a mile wide" and several even more extensive woodlands nearby, whose appeal was enhanced by numerous springs and a "prolific herbage" extending miles and miles to the west. In fact, emphasized Sibley and his crew who had traversed a substantial segment of the same "Great American Desert" that had so negatively impressed both Pike and Long, "in the season of flowers, a very large portion of this great plain presents one continual *carpet* of soft verdure, enriched by flowers of every tint."[9]

Interestingly, certainly from the perspective of the government's plan to prepare the way for a permanent Indian country west of

Missouri, the camping and hunting agreements included in the Santa Fe Trail treaties with the Kansas and the Osages were in fact superfluous at the time of their negotiation. In his journal entry for August 11, 1825, Sibley wrote, "The [Kansa] chiefs & principal men all went away [from Sora Kansas Creek] perfectly satisfied, as well they might, for the right of way through the country claimed by them as their right, is at best a doubtful one, if the Treaty lately signed by them at St. Louis with General Clark is ratified and confirmed by Congress."[10] It is all but certain that the Kansa leaders who signed at Sora Kansas Creek (and possibly the Osages at Council Grove as well) were unaware that Clark had already secured the cession of 20,000,000 acres from the two tribes, encompassing most of the Santa Fe Trail hinterland from Missouri to the Mexican boundary.

In his letter of transmittal accompanying the treaties to the War Department, Clark insisted that the Kansas had been well represented at the negotiations, "the Chiefs with a party of warriors from every village being present and fully authorized before they left home according to their discretions."[11] But that was not the case. In fact there was only one Kansa village in 1825, and the division into three separate villages did not occur until 1829 at the earliest and then mainly because of intratribal bickering over the details of the St. Louis treaty.[12] Moreover, the Kansa leaders who granted the Santa Fe Trail concessions were not the leaders who had negotiated with Clark three months earlier. Clark did not attend the Sora Kansas Creek meeting in August 1825, and Shonegenega—the principal Kansa chief in 1825—signed at Sora Kansas Creek but not at St. Louis. Nompawarah, the mixed-blood advocate who with the support of Clark and other Indian Office officials in St. Louis was in the process of challenging Shonegenega as the dominant Kansa leader in 1825, signed at St. Louis but not at Sora Kansas Creek. The elderly and distinguished Wakanzare, who had signed a peace and friendship treaty with the United States in 1815 and who in the meantime had broken away from the Nompawarah faction while remaining supportive of Shonegenega as a means of protesting the massive Kansa land cession in 1825, signed neither of the agreements.[13]

The only federal official present at all the deliberations was George C. Sibley. He was in St. Louis on June 2 and 3, 1825, at Council Grove on August 10, 1825, and at Sora Kansas Creek on August 16, 1825. He was a veteran of the government's factory system of trade and a seasoned explorer who had traveled through future Indian country and had observed its topography and resources firsthand, from the Missouri frontier to the Pawnee villages in present-day northern Kansas and southern Nebraska and the Grand Saline far to the south. He had also attempted, albeit unsuccessfully, to open an area west of Fort Osage extending into the eastern flank of future Indian country—an area he characterized as the "Garden of Missouri"—to white settlement as early as September 1818. In the summer of 1825, he and his fellow commissioners had surveyed and marked the American portion of the Santa Fe Trail for the benefit of international merchants and domestic travelers alike and by treaty had secured valuable rights-of-way from what Congress had termed the "intervening tribes of Indians."[14] It was a not inconsiderable achievement as well as a portent of important changes in the Indian country to come.

In Washington, chief clerk for Indian affairs Thomas L. McKenney was elated with the land cessions secured by Superintendent Clark. To Secretary of War James Barbour he wrote:

> A judicious arrangement as to space between those two [Osage and Kansa] reservations, and between the frontier of Missouri has been effected . . . and a country, represented to be fertile, and in all respects desirable, provided, and in sufficient extent,

beyond the boundaries of Missouri and Arkansas, for the accommodation of all the tribes within the States, which, should they incline to occupy it, it is the policy of the Government to guarantee to them lasting and undisturbed possession.[15]

"Lasting and undisturbed possession" as a carrot for luring eastern Indians west was not unlike Potawatomi Chief Quish-Queh-Leh's plea to President Jackson a decade later to have his people "enclosed within a strong fence."[16] As an essential component of the government's removal policy it conformed well with Clark's decision to locate the new Osages and Kansas reserves well beyond the western boundary of Missouri, thus "preventing a white and Indian population from remaining in immediate contact with each other." Indeed, emphasized Clark in a letter to Secretary Barbour soon after the St. Louis treaties had been finalized, the Indians themselves were "fully sensible of the inconveniences of such neighborhoods."[17]

Neither Clark nor McKenney advised Barbour of the particular details of the right-of-way treaties that were bound to have a negative effect on emigrant Indians such as the Missouri Shawnees, who by 1825 had already surrendered their lands in southeastern Missouri for a much-diminished reservation directly in the path of the Santa Fe Trail commerce. Nor did Clark and McKenney stress to Barbour that the substance of the statute authorizing the treaties only allowed for (1) the marking of the road from the western boundary of Missouri to the Mexican boundary and (2) the "consent of the intervening Indians, by treaty, to the marking of said road, and to the unmolested use thereof of the citizens of the United States and Mexico." In fact, the marking of the road beyond the international boundary required additional negotiations between the United States and Mexico.[18] But as has been noted, the Sibley commission added the subsistence and camping articles to both treaties on its own, articles that neither McKenney nor Clark and not even the

Senate chose to question and articles that clearly prepared the way for the legal threat Kiowa-Comanche Agent Jesse H. Leavenworth experienced at Fort Zarah three decades later. Was his experience at the hands of trader Dietz little more than a frivolous threat with no legal merit? Or was the purveyor of illegal strong spirits simply seeking to protect his property from Agent Leavenworth's illegal intrusion while the trader was camping near the Santa Fe Trail under protection of the Osage and Kansas right-of-way treaties of 1825?

Well in advance of the opening of the Santa Fe Trail (and the Kansa-Osage land cessions that followed), President Monroe had informed Congress (on December 2, 1817) that "the earth was given to support the greatest number of which it is capable and no tribe or people had a right to withhold from the wants of others more than is necessary for their own support and comfort."[19] It was a clarion call for removing myriad Indians from the east to the trans-Mississippi West, a call that seven years later had become a matter "of very high importance to our Union," in the words of Monroe in his annual message to Congress on January 27, 1825.[20]

That matter, of course, was the unrelenting pressure exerted by white farmers and their political representatives from the Ohio Valley to the Deep South to remove Indians from their ancestral homes and, more specifically, to deal with an immediate land crisis involving the Creek nation, the state of Georgia, and the federal government dating back to 1802. In short, the perceived locus of the Indian problem was in the East, not the West, and although the circumstances of western tribes such as the Osages and Kansas were possibly seen as related and perhaps even integral to a likely solution, they clearly were not the problem itself. With a new legal definition of Indian country in the offing, however, that perception would change dramatically.

The Creek problem, which resulted from white planter encroachment onto Creek lands, dating back to the eighteenth century, became dramatically more complicated in 1802 when the federal government negotiated an agreement with Georgia state officials whereby Georgia agreed to cede its western land claims to the United States on condition that the United States extinguish the title of every acre of Indian land within the borders of Georgia, and with the further understanding that such action would be accomplished as peacefully as possible and on reasonable terms. But with the Creeks' titles still intact as late as 1824 and the posture of white farmers and merchants in west-central Georgia becoming increasingly bellicose, an emergency land cession council was convened on December 7, 1824, at Broken Arrow, near the Alabama state line. There U.S. negotiator Duncan G. Campbell bluntly informed the Creek leaders that they had to sell all of their Georgia lands and take up residence on new lands set aside for them west of the Mississippi River.[21] The majority of the Creeks were vehemently opposed to relinquishing their homeland, which predated the invasion of the Georgians in 1732, and Campbell himself admitted that the so-called arrangement would have to await action by the federal government "to buy them a tract from a western tribe," thus admitting that in fact no such tract was available as of December 7, 1824, the date of the council.[22]

In response to a possible impasse, Missouri Senator Thomas Hart Benton, chairman of the Senate Committee on Indian Affairs, introduced a bill on February 1, 1825, authorizing the president to obtain land from the western Indians to provide new homes for Indians in general who might relinquish title to their lands in the East for comparable lands in the West. If signed into law, it would, of course, provide accommodations for the Creeks. But Benton and his Missouri constituency had more in mind than simply providing relief for the citizens of Georgia. On May 14, 1824, Benton presented to the Senate a memorial entitled "Proposition to Extinguish Indian Title to Lands in Missouri, drawn up by the General Assembly of the state of Missouri. The Indians in question were designated "remnants" of the Shawnees, Delawares, Piankashaws, Peorias, Kickapoos, and Osages, that is, Indians whose continued residence in certain "small districts" in Missouri was "pregnant with evil to both the Indians themselves, and to the people of Missouri." Fortunately, the Osage and Kansa claims to an enormous body of land west of Missouri and Arkansas were "merely nominal," according to Benton. In fact, read the memorial, these tribes actually occupied no more than four or five core village sites. All the remaining acreage of an estimated several hundred thousand square miles was "idle" or used for hunting, and was becoming "less valuable with the daily decrease of game." Moreover, the Missouri Indians were fully sensible of their precarious position. Indeed, insisted Benton and his crowd, these unfortunate natives had too long suffered from "the contact and pressure of a white population" to remain culturally viable and were too few in number to ward off the "moral and physical" forces leading to their tragic degradation.[23]

Even so, and certainly with no assurances (or possible awareness) that the amount of land required to accommodate the large Creek population was legally unavailable in the homeland of the Kansas, Osages, and Pawnees, Commissioners Campbell and James Meriwether, representing the United States, and the "duly authorized" headmen of the Creek tribe signed what turned out to be the fraudulent Indian Springs Treaty of February 12, 1825. Although Article 2 of the illicit agreement promised the Creeks land, "acre for acre, westward of the Mississippi, on the Arkansas river"—essentially the land bisected by the only recently opened Santa Fe Trail—Article 4 provided that if the Arkansas country was deemed unacceptable by the Creeks, they could have "any other territory west of the Mississippi, on [the] Red, Canadian, Arkansas, or Missouri Rivers—the territories of the Cherokees and Choctaws excepted; and if the territory so to be selected shall be in the occupancy of other Indian tribes, then the United States will extinguish the title of such occupants for the benefit of said emigrants."[24]

Insofar as it related to the promise of a new Indian country in the West, the overriding phrase was "will extinguish the title of such occupants [the Osages and Kansas] for the benefit of said emigrants [the Creeks].[25] Thus when Clark forwarded the St. Louis cession treaties to the War Department for Senate confirmation, he could rest confident that he had addressed the expectations of both Commissioner Duncan and the Creek negotiators at Indian Springs in distant Georgia, and that the treaties had opened the door "*for other tribes in different states* [emphasis added] who may be willing to remove to the West in pursuance of the system for the gradual removal and collocation of Indians" as well. The ceded land west of Missouri, reported Clark, was "wonderfully adapted" to native improvement in general and adoption of the white man's way of life.[26]

In addition to these accolades there were other no less persuasive inducements for both Indian *and* white occupation west of Missouri and Arkansas in the decade preceding 1834. The most essential objective written into the federal statute of March 3, 1819, "An Act Making Provision for the Civilization of the Indian Tribes Adjoining the Frontier Settlements,[27] was the promotion of "civilization" among the tribes by means of appropriations, to be awarded to so-called benevolent white societies that thereby would educate the Indians and rescue them from their moral depravity and instruct them in the techniques of white agriculture and land speculation. More often than not these federal "civilization" grants led to the establishment of Christian mission schools in or near the Indians' main villages or camping sites, and to the granting of land or the value thereof, usually by inclusion in a formal treaty, to a particular "civilizing" denomination.[28]

The United Foreign Mission Society (UFMS) was one of the first Protestant organizations to enter into the new federal program. Less than three months after the Civilization Act became law, the UFMS dispatched the Reverend Epaphras Chapman and Job P. Vinall on an exploratory mission to the lower Arkansas River valley, which was followed by a larger delegation led by the Reverend William F. Vaill to a site on the banks of the Neosho (or Grand) River 20 miles north of the present Muskogee, Oklahoma. Named Union, it was the first publicly subsidized "civilizing" mission in the future Oklahoma, and it soon spawned additional efforts to reshape the life of the Osages. It also paved the way for a significant non-Indian advance into future Indian country.[29]

During the following summer Osage Chief White Hair and a delegation of his supporters journeyed to Washington, where they petitioned Superintendent McKenney to extend the Union experiment to what was designated Harmony Mission on the Little Osage River 10 miles west of present-day Nevada, Missouri, near the eastern boundary of the Osage cession of 1825. It was an exceptionally fine settlement location, according to missionary reports. With its abundance of hardwood timber, ample supply of building stone, natural mill-seat location in the Little Osage, and thousands of acres of nearby prairie "fit for the scythe," Harmony in early 1822, the missionaries reported, was a place where "never had people more reason to admire the goodness of God toward them."[30] Three years later a mission outpost of Harmony was established far into the region that would become Indian country, on the banks of the Neosho River 100 miles southeast of Council Grove. There the Reverend Benton Pixley, in company with his family and with the assistance of the federal government, was authorized to learn the Osage language as a means of instructing the Osages in speaking and reading English, ciphering, farming, and accepting the UFMS's essential beliefs regarding group ethics and individual morality.[31]

Unlike Harmony, Mission Neosho was located in the very heart of Osage country and thus more intimately caught up in the internal disputes for control of the Osages' destiny in the 1820s. In January 1825, Superintendent William Clark instructed Osage Agent Alexander McNair to unite the competing bands, but to no immediate avail. McNair's untimely death in the spring of 1826 led to the appointment of John Francis Hamtramck as the replacement Osage agent and to orders for Hamtramck to continue where McNair had left off, that is, to confine and unify all the Osages onto the land reserved for them under the cession treaty engineered by Clark in June 1825.[32]

It was a nearly impossible order, and at Mission Neosho matters deteriorated into a highly competitive and ultimately divisive debacle. Hamtramck's efforts at unification apparently infringed on the UFMS's program at Neosho and clearly angered the resident missionaries there, particularly Pixley, who accused the new Osage agent of frequent and extended absences from Neosho. But there was more. Hamtramck was also charged with hiring incompetent agriculturists and blacksmiths who pocketed their salaries while providing little or no service to the Indians, and worse. According to Pixley and fellow missionary Samuel B. Bright, the federal agent had engaged in "illicit and adulterous intercourse" with the Indian women during the limited time that he was in residence at Neosho. Hamtramck's response was that "the greatest good they [the UFMS missionaries] have done is providing themselves a large and productive farm." That the farm was productive is confirmed by the 250 bushels of corn harvested during the first year of the mission's operation, but whether the grain was used for the exclusive benefit of the Indians or whites (or for both) is not clear. Still, the mission society board did report that as a result of the bountiful crop at Neosho in 1826, "the expense of supporting the mission families was very moderate." Superintendent Clark attempted to mend fences between Hamtramck and the missionaries, but did not succeed, and Mission Neosho and the farm were closed in the spring of 1829.[33]

There were other non-Indian farm operations in future Indian country, including the one operated by Methodist Episcopal teacher Thomas Sears Huffaker among the Kansas at Council Grove. In 1857, several years after Huffaker had retired from his government post and had turned to farming and land development on his own, a delegation of angry Kansas told Indian Commissioner James W. Denver in Washington that Huffaker was a "bad missionary . . . who didn't teach anything," a stern taskmaster who forced fifty young Kansas to work in his two fields "the size of Washington." The corn and other produce from these fields, said Kansa delegates Hard Hart, White Hair, and The Wolf to Commissioner Denver, were for the benefit of white settlers in the Council Grove area, not the Indians.[34]

Whether such missionary teachers and their "agriculturist" assistants were more interested in tribal land than their assigned task of cultivating the Indians' moral and economic well-being, as a prominent Osage historian has written, is problematic.[35] In the case of the Potawatomi removal treaty of 1846, it was clearly stipulated that the "missionary establishment" authorized by the government revert back to Potawatomi "use" in the event that its land was no longer being used for its original "civilizing" purpose.[36] In contrast, the Omaha treaty of 1854 granted 640 acres of Omaha land outright to the Board of Foreign Missions of the Presbyterian Church "so as to include as near as may be all the improvements heretofore made by them."[37] Although some of these so-called benevolent societies were able to report the kind of cultural changes the government believed would lead to general native improvement,[38] they also generated a plethora of publicity regarding the easy access, the inviting climate, and, of course, the fertile terrain awaiting non-Indian farmers and speculators.

No better example of this arousing of interest was the experience of the Missouri Shawnees, first of the emigrant tribes to be relocated in the region designated Indian country in 1834. On November 7, 1825, Superintendent Clark negotiated a treaty whereby the Missouri Shawnees relinquished title to all their lands in the vicinity of Cape Girardeau, in southeastern Missouri, in return for a $25,000 cash payment for improvements left behind and spoliation claims against citizens of the United States, and a 50-mile-square tract west of Missouri located "within the purchase lately made from the Osages" in what is now southeastern Kansas or, if they so chose, an equal quantity of land north or south of the Kansas River due west of the Missouri state line.[39] The tribe as a whole opted for the Kansas River location because of its strategic location at the confluence of the Missouri and Kansas rivers, and most settled on the more fertile south side of the Kansas River, where within the next few years they were joined by additional Shawnees from Ohio, including the Wapakonetas and the Fish band to which the families of Tecumseh and the Prophet belonged.[40]

These emigrant Shawnees became the object of intense solicitation by missionaries of the Baptist and Methodist Episcopal churches. Chief Paschal Fish had voiced a preference for the Methodists as early as 1830, and that same year the Reverend Isaac McCoy had suggested to a Shawnee tribal council that the Baptists deserved consideration because of apparent Methodist indecision. The Wapakoneta Shawnee chiefs in Ohio, however, voiced a preference for the Society of Friends, whom they considered more trustworthy as they confronted the prospect of a new and unsettled life in the trans-Missouri West. All these Christian denominations, of course, were anxious to secure government assistance for their efforts.[41]

In the meantime, intruders from nearby Missouri occupied portions of the Shawnee reservation in the fall of 1834, prompting the Shawnees "in full council" to demand the immediate removal of all unauthorized Indians, missionaries, and settlers on their lands.[42]

Shawnee Subagent Marston G. Clark tried to comply by requesting help from Colonel Henry Dodge at Fort Leavenworth, located only a few miles north of the Shawnee lands. But Dodge denied the subagent's request on grounds that he needed direct orders from his superiors for such a bold action. Whether Dodge actually requested help from Washington is not known; what is known is that there was no military expulsion of the intruders. A few months later it was reported that several white families had moved into the area between the Missouri state line and the Missouri River—the so-called Platte Purchase area of present-day northwestern Missouri—and it was in response to this incursion that Superintendent William Clark in effect concurred with Colonel Dodge's evasive response to Subagent Clark. Noting that "many more" families were bound to come, Superintendent Clark explained to the Indian commissioner in Washington, "Should it be considered proper to have these persons removed—a point which I should suppose will mainly depend on the disposition made or intended to be made, of the country in question, the removal can I apprehend only be effected by a military force acting under direct orders of the President."[43] Subagent Clark had resigned in the meantime, citing the Shawnees' lack of confidence in him as a government official with the responsibility of protecting them from outside exploitation, and especially his "inability to control traders, trappers, missionaries, whiskey smugglers, and Santa Feeans."[44] Thus the intruder problem remained unresolved until it was worsened by the advent of even more aggressive intruders, particularly in the early 1850s, and a developing consensus that the 1834 law was not an insurmountable obstacle to non-Indian settlement in Indian country.

Still others were preparing the way. On May 25, 1824, President Monroe signed a law authorizing $10,000 for the funding of a commission to negotiate treaties of peace and friendship with the several Indian tribes then resident along the upper Missouri River and on the northern plains. Usually referred to as the Yellowstone Expedition because of its itinerary to the area just beyond the mouth of the Yellowstone, the expedition was led by Brevet Brigadier General Henry Atkinson and Benjamin O'Fallon, with the former serving as expedition commander. It was a successful venture for Atkinson, and shortly after his return to St. Louis in late October 1825, he was asked by General Jacob Brown, commanding general of the army, to submit his views on Indian removal and military security along the Santa Fe Trail as well as the western frontier in general. Atkinson's response was supportive of removal but with the cautionary recommendation that a line of forts be established for protecting the settlements along "the whole extent of the [Indian] country" and for promoting peace among the various tribes while protecting them from abuse and exploitation by the invading whites.[45]

General Atkinson's recommendations for a permanent and secure home for the removal Indians were certainly heartening to Indian Office strategists in the War Department, but in 1825 there were a number of forts in or near where the removal Indians were destined to reside. As early as 1816, for example, Fort Armstrong had been built on an island in the Mississippi between present-day Rock Island, Illinois, and Davenport, Iowa; Fort Snelling, at the confluence of the Minnesota and Mississippi rivers in present-day Minnesota, had been constructed in 1819. Both facilities were given important responsibilities for adjudicating differences between Indian people and the white settlers. General Atkinson himself had established Fort Atkinson on the west bank of the Missouri River a few miles north of the present Omaha that same year, and in 1817 Fort Smith had been constructed on the banks of the Arkansas River near the western boundary of Arkansas. Forts Gibson, Coffee, and Towson, all official military installations with important responsibilities on the so-called Indian frontier, had been established in eastern Oklahoma as early as 1824.[46]

One major military installation that came into existence as a direct result of Atkinson's recommendation to the War Department was Fort Leavenworth (originally Cantonment Leavenworth), erected in the spring of 1827 by Colonel Henry Leavenworth on the west bank of the Missouri River about 25 miles above the mouth of the Kansas River. Originally intended to provide protection for the Santa Fe Trail traders, it soon evolved into a more comprehensive military facility and by midcentury was serving as the general depot for virtually all the government's military operations in Indian country.[47] By virtue of its strategic location on the Missouri River gateway to the very heart of Indian country and, of course, its ever-increasing personnel and material resources, Fort Leavenworth was positioned to exert enormous influence in the preservation of law and order in the trans-Missouri West. But it also housed, fed, and provided employment for certain military personnel who engaged in land and town speculation near Leavenworth's military boundaries not far from the removal reservation established for the Shawnees in 1825. These military speculators apparently viewed themselves as insulated from prosecution and expulsion because of their official duties in Indian country. But as we shall see, nothing in the 1834 law authorized non-Indians, including the military, to enter Indian country for the purpose of building a town, tilling a field, grazing livestock, constructing a road or bridge, or attempting to gain title to land reserved for Indians.[48]

The speculation called attention to the bedrock issue of how Congress and the executive branch contemplated the character of tribal land tenure once the new Indian country became a reality. Toward the end of his second administration President Jefferson had advised a visiting delegation of tribal leaders that it was good public policy for every Indian head of family to have his own farm in fee simple, that is, to cultivate it for himself and his family's benefit, and that after him this farm should be given to his wife and their children with no legal strings attached. Why? Jefferson felt that individual landownership and the prudent cultivation thereof encouraged respect for the law and the elected officials empowered to enforce the law, which in turn encouraged peace and understanding between Indians and non-Indians, and ultimately resulted in the former becoming true and responsible Americans.[49]

Within a decade, however, as Robert W. McCluggage's study of the Senate's authority over Indian land titles has suggested,[50] Jefferson's idealism in the matter had been overruled. Writing to Indian Superintendent William Clark in response to Clark's request for clarification concerning the reservation rights of the Quapaws in the future Arkansas,[51] specifically the Quapaws' rights as "tenants in common" as opposed to their "power to divide it amongst themselves, and the right to dispose thereof, afterwards, separately," Secretary of War John C. Calhoun told Clark on May 8, 1818, "The land reserved for the Quapaws must be held by the [usufruct] tenure by which the Indians usually hold their lands, as the Senate would probably ratify no treaty which recognizes in the Indians the right of acquiring individual property, with the power of selling, except to the United States."[52]

Nevertheless, there were allotments granted in fee simple (but on occasion with other qualifications) to individual Indians before and after 1834.[53] Both the Osage and the Kansa land cession treaties of 1825 contained individual allotments for the "half-breeds" of the two tribes, that is, one section of 640 acres to each of the forty Osage "half-breeds" and a reservation "one mile square" (that is, 640 acres) for each of the twenty-three Kansa "half-breeds." Whereas the Osage allotments were specifically granted for the "*use* [emphasis added] of the half-breeds," the Kansa allotments were simply "made . . . for each of the half-breeds," with no stipulations regarding use.[54] Were the Kansa allotments, all located in future Indian country due west of the new Shawnee reservation, inalienable? Or could they be sold by their "half-breed" owners for a profit, without permission from their great father in Washington? Secretary Calhoun's instructions to William Clark on the Quapaw land question in 1818 notwithstanding, the St. Louis Indian superintendent was still not sure, and it was therefore left to Congress or the courts to issue a final determination.[55] Meanwhile, in a letter accompanying the 1825 Kansa treaty sent to Washington for Senate approval, Clark sought to justify inclusion of the "half-breed" article in the final Kansa treaty draft: "Reserves of this kind have heretofore been made in behalf of such ["half-breed"] persons and in my opinion have a good effect in promoting civilization as their attachment is created for a fixed residence and an idea of separate property is imparted without which it is vain to think of improving the minds and morals of the Indians or making progress in the work of civilization."[56]

4

Promise

After ratification of the Kansa and Osage land cessions prerequisite to the advent of an enlarged and well-defined Indian country, Clark's standing as an authority on Indian affairs in the trans-Missouri West increased dramatically. His celebrated 1804–1806 journey with Meriwether Lewis and the "Corps of Discovery" from the Mississippi River to the mouth of the Columbia provided government dignitaries and the public with new perspectives and valuable data regarding the climate and topography where eastern Indians might establish new homes and, perhaps, even thrive. In addition, his efficient and certainly uncontroversial performance as Indian agent in the vast Louisiana Territory placed him in good standing with his War Department superiors. Writing to the secretary of war within the framework of the mixed-blood allotments he had only recently authorized for the Osages and Kansas, Clark recommended that the government fence individual farm plots for the benefit of those Indians who agreed to take up residence west of the Missouri River. He also called for public assistance in breaking sod for tribal agricultural development, and for fruit trees, stock animals, and assorted fowl, which would enable the Indians to achieve economic security. In the final analysis, insisted Clark, individual property was the key to success. In fact it was individual landownership that had "raised" the southern tribes and enabled them to live independently and "cultivate their minds," while those without such security were consigned to the "lowest state of moral and mental degradation" imaginable.[1]

As Indian agent for the Louisiana Territory from 1807 until his appointment as territorial governor of Missouri in 1813, Clark's main responsibilities were to counteract British influence among the Indians of the middle and upper Missouri country and to encourage Indian farming and social improvement consistent with the Jeffersonian agrarian ideal. But a policy of Indian removal then being discussed both privately and publicly for precisely such purposes was no certain guarantee of tribal survival and acceptance of the white man's way of life, warned Clark. After his appointment to head the St. Louis Indian Superintendency in 1822, however, Clark enthusiastically supported a removal policy that would place thousands of Indians under his administrative control in the trans-Missouri West.[2]

Although the Kansa, Osage, and Shawnee cessions authorized tribal relocations on a limited scale and, in fact, were urged forward by circumstances far removed from the trans-Missouri West, there were harbingers of land grabbing among the removal Indians soon to come. Simply stated, political pressure exerted on the War Department and Congress in the 1820s by agrarian and commercial interests in the South and the trans-Allegheny West called for a sweeping reorganization of Indian affairs and a revised Indian policy that would address the concerns of southern planters and midwestern farmers alike. And with important responsibilities for deciding the character of native improvement in a remote area soon to be designated Indian country, Governor William Clark was more than eager to support the new dispensation.[3]

Achieving these changes required legislative action and the drafting of a proposal or proposals by persons of knowledge and experience in Indian affairs, not just members of a Senate or House
committee who had never been west of the Missouri or an Indian
Office clerk confined to his desk in the nation's capital. Not surprisingly, then, the War Department turned to its two most experienced
field superintendents for the task: William Clark, head of the St.
Louis Superintendency, and Lewis Cass, territorial governor of
Michigan and ex officio head of the Michigan Superintendency. In
the 1820s the St. Louis and Michigan Superintendencies were
among the largest in the country, with jurisdiction over more than
60,000 members of the Osage, Kansa, Omaha, Pawnee, Sac and
Fox, Cheyenne, Arapaho, Kiowa, Comanche, Crow, Sioux, Chippewa, Potawatomi, Ottawa, Winnebago, Menominee, Shawnee,
Delaware, and Miami tribes, thus providing a valuable overview of
the problems facing Indian people at that time. In his July 28, 1828,
letter of appointment to Clark and Cass, Secretary of War Peter B.
Porter praised the two men for their intimate experience on the Indian frontier and pointed out that their understanding of Indian
customs, aspirations, and capabilities would be "peculiarly useful and
desirable" as the government moved toward legislative change in Indian affairs.[4] Like Cass, Clark accepted the assignment with no
equivocation; he observed that "the dictates of humanity & justice,"
enhanced by his myriad experiences in the trans-Mississippi West,
called for a new or substantially revised code for the effective administration of Indian affairs. High on Clark's wish list were laws "explicit and consistent to punish the various descriptions of offenses
which arise within & and without the Country."[5]

For his part in the drafting of new Indian legislation, Lewis Cass
was an energetic but ethnocentric administrator who, in the words
of his most recent biographer, "viewed Indians as barbarous and im-
petuous children who need to be treated with paternal care." He was

a lukewarm supporter of Indian removal in his early years as Michigan superintendent, explaining in 1818 that before Indians would feel obliged to move they would have to be almost completely surrounded by white settlements. And even as late as 1826 he wrote that in some circumstances "it [was] better to do nothing, than to hazard the risk of increasing their [the Indians'] misery" by forcing them to move from their traditional homelands.[6] Nevertheless, in a speech that same year to a party of Potawatomi and Miami leaders gathered by the government on the upper Wabash for the purpose of relinquishing legal title to their traditional lands north of the Ohio and east of the Mississippi, Cass said: "Your Father owns a large country west of the Mississippi. He is anxious that all his red children should remove there. Now is the time to make a good bargain for yourselves which will make you rich and comfortable. Come forward, then, like wise men, and accept the terms we offer."[7] The new country beyond the Mississippi was a land of promise and plenty, said Cass, where Indian people once again might enjoy peace and have a permanent place to live and raise their families. "Your Great Father will not suffer his white children to reside there," was his solemn promise to the Indians, "for it is reserved for the red people; it will be yours as long as the sun shines and the rain falls."[8]

Peace, prosperity, and a permanent place for hundreds or perhaps thousands of emigrant Indians in a place William Clark had simply designated "the Country" were thus the guiding principles of the two superintendents as they proceeded with their assignment in the late summer of 1829. Not unrelated to their deliberations was the first general Indian removal bill, which would be heatedly debated and passed by a slim majority in Congress in the early months of 1830 and signed into law by President Jackson on May 28, 1830. The new statute provided the president with $500,000 for removing Indians who volunteered to "exchange" their lands in the East in favor of "districts" west of the Mississippi River that would be clearly marked off by "natural or artificial marks." None of these "districts" could be situated within the boundaries of any state or organized territory, nor could they be located on land to which the Indian title had not been ceded—hence the crucial importance of the massive Osage and Kansa cessions Clark had secured half a decade earlier. Section 3 of the 1830 law provided further:

> In the making of any such exchange or exchanges, it shall and may be lawful for the President to solemnly assure the tribe or nation with which the exchange is made, that the United States *will forever secure and guaranty to them, and their heirs or successors, the country so exchanged with them* [emphasis added]; and if they prefer it that the United States will cause a patent or grant to be made and executed to them for the same.

Additionally, Section 6 provided that it "shall and may be lawful" for the president to provide the removal Indians with protection "against all interruption or disturbance from any other tribe or nation of Indians, *or from any other person or persons whatever*" (emphasis added).[9]

Whether the architects and advocates of this new law understood or were even aware that the "interruption or disturbance" clause was contrary to the Santa Fe Trail rights-of-way treaties negotiated by Clark five years earlier is not known. But what is known is that by 1830 there had been a dramatic increase in the number of non-Indians traveling, hunting, foraging, and camping in the region where, presumably, the removal districts would soon be located. In the early spring of 1830, for example, the Western Department of the American Fur Company sent an overland expedition of 45 mounted men and a pack train of more than 100 animals from Liberty, Missouri, to the company's trading posts on the western slope of South Pass, in present-day Wyoming. The route was through the very heart of Pawnee country (and the northern rim of Kansa country), and although the 1825 Pawnee treaty prohibited illegal or unlicensed persons from entering their country, it by no means allowed for a legal right-of-way as in the case of the Kansas and Osages along the Santa Fe Trail to the south.[10] Soon thereafter, on April 20, 1830, William L. Sublette's company of 81 mounted men and a caravan of ten wagons and assorted livestock left St. Louis for the Wind River valley in present-day Wyoming. Their route was the Santa Fe Trail about 40 miles west of the Missouri border, at which point they crossed the Kansas River and headed northwest to the Platte, along the same route the American Fur Company expedition had taken a few weeks earlier. A month later, a caravan of 120 men and sixty wagons left Blue Springs, Missouri, for Santa Fe, which they reached without incident on August 4, 1830.[11]

Certainly by the time the 1830 removal bill had been signed, there was no lack of non-Indians camping on and crossing the area soon to "receive"—as the 1830 bill phrased it—Indians, and as traffic increased over what by the mid-1830s had been termed the Oregon Trail, Indian agents reported the Indians' increasing anxiety and concern over the "wanton destruction of game, the firing of the prairie, and other injuries." The situation had worsened so much by 1848 that St. Louis Indian Superintendent Thomas H. Harvey warned that "bloody encounters, if not outright wars of extermination," were possible if the destructive intrusions of the overlanders west of Missouri and Iowa were not contained. Of special concern to the Indians, said Harvey, was the government's obligation to negotiate a right-of-way agreement through their Platte Valley domain.[12]

But that call for action was in the future. The task at hand was for Clark and Cass to provide the War Department with a proposal encompassing "the whole range of Indian affairs" while offering revisions in policy and procedure acceptable to the Jacksonian plan for major change in Indian policy. Their report, composed of fifty-six sections and entitled "An act for regulating trade and intercourse with the Indian Tribes and for the general management of Indians affairs," was submitted to Secretary of War Porter in early February 1829. In his letter of transmittal to the Senate, Porter thanked Clark and Cass for their good work and recommended that their report "receive the early consideration to which its merits, in the opinion of the Department, entitle it."[13]

The bill submitted to Porter (and Congress) included copies or summary transcriptions of laws in effect for some time as well as new proposals, including the need for an Indian commissioner to be assigned to the War Department, the importance of trade licenses and passports for non-Indian travel into Indian country, and more stringent penalties for selling, bartering, or simply distributing alcohol to Indians. To most of these proposals was attached a review of the historical context and justifications that capsulated Clark's and Cass's thinking, for example, the very important Section 28, which proposed a new definition of the boundary line of sundry Indian nations whose lands were legally determined by treaties with the United States.[14] The old boundary, described in a fifty-two-line paragraph in the Indian Trade and Intercourse Act of March 30, 1802, extended from the mouth of the Cuyahoga River at Lake Erie in an increasingly varied line south to the middle of St. Mary's River on the present Georgia-Florida border. The section included the stipulation "that if the boundary line between said Indian tribes and the United States shall, at any time hereafter, be varied, by any treaty which shall be made between the said Indian tribes and the United States, then *all* [emphasis added] provisions contained in this act shall be construed to apply to said line so to be varied, in the same manner as said provisions apply, by force of this act, to the boundary line herein before recited."[15]

Thus if the boundary of a particular Indian nation were altered by treaty after March 30, 1802, more than a score of stipulations included in the 1802 act might or might not be enforceable within the confines of new land awarded to the Indian nation in question, including the death penalty as provided in Section 6 of the 1802 act for non-Indians convicted of murdering an Indian in any "town, settlement or territory belonging to any nation or tribe of Indians." It therefore mattered a great deal regarding precisely where the boundaries of Indian land were at a particular time, as treaty after treaty rendered the Indian country line more and more difficult to describe. In fact, emphasized Clark and Cass in their 1829 report, the various land cessions after 1802 had "so totally changed this line, that no part of it now constitutes a boundary" and that it had become "tedious to describe." Consequently, in Section 28 of their report of 1829, Clark and Cass simply proposed:

> that the limits of the several cessions which have been made to the United States, by the Indian tribes when the same divide the possessions of the said tribe from the United States, shall be the boundary line between said tribes and the United States. And, as future cessions may be made, the said boundary line shall be moved to, and correspond therewith. And the said line *shall be clearly marked and ascertained, in all such places as the President of the United States may deem necessary, and in such manner as he may direct.*[16]

Although the 1802 act did call for the marking of treaty boundaries in a manner the president deemed necessary, it clearly was not accentuated in the manner Clark and Cass opted for nearly three decades later, underscoring the fact that by 1829 the boundaries of Indian country had become a much more important issue than in 1802. Writing to Cass on November 19, 1831, less than three months after President Jackson had appointed Cass to head the War Department, Commissioner of Indian Affairs Elbert Herring attributed the desire for a more precise perception and delineation of Indian country not to the interests of the Indians but to "the increase of our [white] population, and the extension of our [white] settlements."[17]

And well he might. Less than two months after the removal bill passed, Clark and Morgan Willoughby met with the Confederated Sacs and Foxes, Omahas, Ioways, Otoes, and Missourias, and the Medawah-Kanton, Wahpacoota, Wahpeton, and Sisston bands of Sioux at Prairie du Chien, and, with annuities and other awards crafted for the promotion of civilization among the Indians whose leaders congregated there, secured title to the western quarter of present-day Iowa and the triangular area north of modern Kansas City between the Platte and Missouri rivers. The intent, according to the treaty, was to provide a permanent living area for those tribes "living thereon, or to such other tribes as the President may locate thereon for hunting, and other purposes."[18] In response, the white residents of western Missouri dispatched a memorial to Congress in which they vehemently opposed the Prairie du Chien agreement.[19]

The Missouri petitioners, however, could take some comfort in that Clark and Cass had called attention to Section 19 of the Indian Trade and Intercourse Act of 1802, which provided that nothing in that act precluded trade and intercourse with Indians, so long as the Indians in question were living on lands within the jurisdiction of any of the several states and "surrounded by white settlements." In fact, said Clark and Cass in their 1829 report, an Indiana District Court had interpreted Section 19 of the 1802 act as follows:

the words "Indian country," *ex vi termini,* mean the country to which the title has not yet been extinguished; and therefore, that many of the provisions of the law apply to Indian camps and settlements, in the country usually occupied by the Indians, and to which the white settlements have not yet extended, although the title may have been ceded to the United States. . . . It would hence appear, that the fact of the Indians living within the ordinary jurisdiction of any of the individual States, was not sufficient to exclude the operation of the [1802] act, but that they must be surrounded by settlements of white persons also.[20]

Although Clark and Cass offered no evaluation and certainly no recommendation for incorporating the Indiana ruling into a new or amended trade and intercourse act, the implicit warning was that devising a new and more intelligible definition of Indian country would be no easy matter.

As we have seen, outgoing Secretary of War Porter recommended that Congress give "early consideration" to the Clark-Cass report, while in the Indian Office head clerk Thomas McKenney termed it "able and judicious" and the draft bill accompanying the report as "ample" for dealing with the matters at hand. Congress, however, deferred action and it fell to the executive branch to carry the ball. Lewis Cass, only days after his appointment as secretary of war (November 19, 1831), submitted his first annual report. After a rambling and drawn-out discussion of national versus state constitutional authority over Indian affairs and a discussion of the government's moral obligation to promote native well-being, Cass offered both question and answer to one of the central issues of the day: "Shall they [the Indians] be advised to remain or remove? If the former, their fate is written in the annals of their race; if the latter, we may yet hope to see them renovated in character and condition by our example and instruction, and by their exertions." From this it plainly followed that a "change of residence . . . from their present positions to the regions west of the Mississippi, presents the only hope of permanent establishment and improvement." And of utmost importance to the success of this humane venture, said Cass, the national government should solemnly declare that "the country assigned to the Indians shall be theirs as long as they or their descendants may occupy it; and a corresponding determination that our settlements shall not spread over it; and every effort should be used to satisfy the Indians of our sincerity and of their security. Without this indispensable preliminary . . . their change of position would bring no change of circumstance."[21]

Two weeks later, in response to mounting political pressure for implementation of the removal law and the establishment of a well-defined and permanent Indian country for the benefit of the removal tribes, President Jackson assured Congress that within a few years the native titles to all lands lying within the several states would be extinguished and the government would remove all Indians unwilling to submit to its laws. "What the native savages become when surrounded by a dense population and by mixing with the whites," said Jackson, "may be seen in the miserable remnants of a few Eastern tribes without political or civil rights . . . dragging out a wretched existence, without excitement, without hope, and almost without thought." But in a distant and protective Indian country, continued Jackson, secular philanthropists and Christian advocates alike would be welcome to "proceed unmolested in the interesting experiment of gradually advancing a community of American Indians from barbarism to the habits and enjoyments of civilized life."[22]

Nevertheless, it was believed that the ubiquitous liquor merchants would enter the promised land and ply their lethal commodity as effectively and profitably as they had done in the past. Thus in a move to fence off the Indians from outside influences, Congress enacted a new prohibition law, in the summer of 1832, decreeing that "no ardent spirits shall be hereafter introduced, under any pretense, into the Indian country,"[23] which conformed well with the views of both Clark and Cass. Only a few months prior to enactment of the 1832 statute Clark had advised Indian Commissioner Elbert Herring that not an Indian among a thousand could be found who after his first drink would not murder to gratify his passion for alcohol,[24] while Cass was on record as having said that native inebriety of "the young and the old, the male and the female, the chief and the warrior" was so brutal and excessive that "human nature in all its variety of aspects presents no phenomenon like this."[25]

But the 1832 law provided no new penalties, and thus the only punishment for convicted violators was that written into an 1822 law allowing Indian agents, territorial governors, and military officers to search for and to seize ardent spirits taken into Indian country.[26] Moreover, the locus of Indian country remained cloudy, and precisely who was denied the right to trade or distribute alcohol under the new law remained unclear as well. In a letter to Secretary Cass soon after the 1832 law went into effect, Osage Agent P. L. Chouteau complained:

> The Kansa Indians have been in the habit of introducing whiskey into this [Osage] nation, which they have sold to the Osages. The Osages are in the habit of paying high for the whiskey introduced. Sometimes a horse for a bottle of whiskey or two. . . . I have not interfered in this traffic as I had not particular instructions and I believe the U.S. Indian Agents generally do not interfere when liquor is introduced into Indian Country by Indians. . . . If it is the intention of Government to prevent the introduction of spirituous liquors altogether the law must operate against Indians as well as the whites. I thus ask—has an Indian Countryman the privilege of introducing liquor in Indian Country?[27]

No response from Secretary Cass was forthcoming, possibly because Agent Chouteau's query was symptomatic of the kinds of problems that might soon be resolved by new and more forceful legislation.

The report of the Stokes Commission, authorized by the government in 1832 to assess conditions in the West for the Five Civilized
Tribes and other emigrant Indians as well as to recommend plans for
tribal government, agriculture development, and general native improvement, was submitted to Congress in the spring of 1834 and was
of considerable importance in fleshing out the dimensions and character of a new Indian country, even though Commissioner Henry
Ellsworth cautioned Secretary Cass that, contrary to Isaac McCoy's
recent description of the area west of Missouri as "habitable" to the
ninety-eighth meridian, more than half of the lands north of the
Osage lands (as defined by the Osage Treaty of 1825) was in fact un-
suitable for agriculture. Furthermore, reported Ellsworth, "There is
not much land below the Platte, until you approach the branches of
the Kanzas River, calculated for agricultural settlement . . . [and] the
general scarcity of wood on the unappropriated tract south of the
Platte will deter most emigrating tribes from making a selection
there."[28] Cass may have been concerned with the contents of the letter. But since there is no record of his response to Ellsworth or any
other government official,[29] Cass more than likely disregarded it as
an inconsequential endnote to the commission's otherwise optimistic report.

In concert with the Clark-Cass recommendations of 1829, then,
the work of the Stokes Commission provided direction for the
House Committee on Indian Affairs to move more confidently toward the design and creation of a new Indian country that once and
for all would accommodate the burgeoning land requirements of the
new removal program. Thus on May 20, 1834, the committee submitted a bill calling for a new territory for Indians that could with-
stand any challenge to the constitutional power of Congress to
dispose of territory belonging to the United States. The aboriginal
title to the contemplated "Western Territory" had been wholly extinguished, said the committee, and the boundaries of the proposed

132,295,680-acre tract—a map of which was submitted with the bill—were the western boundaries of Arkansas and Missouri on the east, the Platte River on the north, and the Mexican possessions on the south and west. And for congressmen receptive to Commissioner Ellsworth's gloomy description of the proposed territory, the House committee insisted that "the soil and climate [west of Missouri and Arkansas] are all that can be desired to reward industry, and to prolong life." Finally, the committee promised that the Western Territory would be "dedicated to the use of the Indian tribes forever." In fact, so resolute was the guarantee that "even to the Indian it [was] as clear and well defined as the edge of the circle of the sun."[30]

Accompanying the "Western (Indian) Territory" bill were two additional bills: one a fairly typical Office of Indian Affairs bill calling for less costly and more efficient operations in Washington and on the frontier, and one for a new trade and intercourse act that would better protect and promote the interests of Indians who took up new homes in the West. The Indian office and the Indian Trade and Intercourse bills passed with little difficulty, mainly because what they called for in terms of administrative improvement and housekeeping measures did not amount to a radical departure from the past.[31]

But with the "Western [Indian] Territory" bill it was a different matter. In spite of the committee's thorough and diplomatic presentation, spearheaded by Horace Everett, of Vermont, the bill failed not by the counting of yeas and nays but by its consignment to the table for a silent death.[32] Leading the anti–Western Territory bill forces was former president John Quincy Adams, who three years earlier had returned to the political arena to represent his native Massachusetts in Congress. The words of a former president could carry much weight, as surely was the case on June 25, 1834, when he announced on the House floor that although "he had never read either the bill or report before today," he nevertheless was certain that

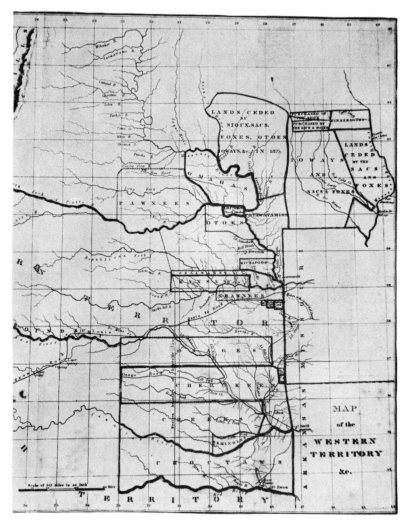

Southeast section of "Map of the [proposed] Western Territory, &c," accompanying *House Report* no. 474 (May 20, 1834) 23: 1, serial 263, reprinted
in Louise Barry, comp., *The Beginning of the West: Annals of the Kansas Gateway to the American West, 1540–1854* (Topeka: Kansas State Historical Society, 1972), 404. Courtesy Kansas State Historical Society.

the proposed Western Territory bill was a violation of the Constitution of 1789.[33] Two decades earlier, in treaty negotiations leading to the end of the War of 1812, Adams had objected to the British attempt to establish an Indian state in the upper Ohio Valley.[34] Now, in 1834, he insisted that the proposed Western (Indian) Territory

> was totally different from any thing that had ever been done before. Did the honorable chairman [Representative Everett] find this right in that clause of the constitution which declares that Congress shall regulate the territories? What were these Territories? They were portions of land and water—inanimate matter. But what right did such a clause give to Congress over human beings? The clause spoke of "The Territories and other property of the United States." Were human beings the "property of the United States," although in a savage condition? Surely not. They were not the "Territories" referred to in the constitution. If the constitution had said, Congress shall have power to regulate human beings as property of the United States, the House would soon have had the question upon the bill. If such a right did exist, why did it not apply to the South, as well as to the Indians of the West?[35]

The former president also decried the "disposition to transfer powers of the Congress to the Executive,"[36] after which Congressman William S. Archer of Virginia elaborated on certain matters of race and territorial expansion:

> If it was in the power of the gentleman [Congressman Everett] from Vermont to add to our Union men of blood and color alien to the people of the United States, where was that right to stop? Why not introduce our brethren of Cuba and

Hayti? . . . You have granted this privilege to the copper colored tribes beyond the Mississippi, can you now deny it to the
deeper colored race who sprang from your own soil? It might
be as great an advantage to have a State in Africa, and a State
in Cuba, and a State in Canada, as a State at the foot of the
Rocky mountains.[37]

Congressman Everett responded rationally and respectfully, but to
no avail. The debate was briefly renewed and then terminated by
Lewis Williams of North Carolina who, "to prevent further consumption of time in debate," moved to lay the bill on the table.
Everett countered with a request for the yeas and nays but was
turned down, and the motion to table carried without a count. And
so the bill to establish a "Western [Indian] Territory" was placed on
the table, from which position it was not removed during the re-
mainder of the Twenty-Third Congress.[38] Subsequent efforts to res-
urrect it were no more successful, and as an actuality the new Indian
country became what was set forth in Section 1 of the 1834 Indian
Trade and Intercourse Act: "That all that part of the United States
west of the Mississippi, not within the states of Missouri and Louisiana, or the territory of Arkansas, and also, that part of the United
States east of the Mississippi River, and not within any state to
which the Indian title has not been extinguished, for the purposes of
this act, be taken and deemed to be the Indian country."[39]

It was an unambiguous definition of a space whose boundaries
presumably were understood by those who voted to create it. But for
the new Indian country to become a place of tribal survival and re-
newal, or an extension of the American empire, or a mix of the two,
it was unavoidable that the movement of hundreds, perhaps thousands of people into the sparsely populated region west of the Missouri would prompt the establishment of new and more elaborate
regulations than in the past, so that, as Felix S. Cohen wrote more

than half a century ago, Indian country was no more and no less than a place within which existing Indian laws and customs and/or existing federal laws relating to Indians at any particular time were generally and legally applicable.[40]

It is not surprising, then, that Congress attached an almost dizzying array of new regulations for both Indian and non-Indian conduct in the new setting, for example, regulations dealing with trade and licensing, barter, trapping, cattle driving, intrusion, land alienation, disturbing the peace, destruction of property, depredations, passports, judicial authority, and, most important of all, a dramatic stiffening of penalties for persons who might "sell, exchange, or give, barter, or dispose of, any spirituous liquor or wine to an Indian (in the Indian country)."[41] There were good reasons for tightening the Indian liquor code in 1834. In that year, about 600 miles west of Missouri but well within the bounds of the new Indian country, Charles Bent and Ceran St. Vrain completed the construction of a large adobe trading post on the dry route of the Santa Fe Trail near present-day La Junta, Colorado. That same year also, William, Charles's older brother, joined with Charles and St. Vrain to organize the firm of Bent, St. Vrain and Company, which on December 13, 1834 (under the names of Charles Bent and twenty-nine of the firm's employees), was granted a license by the St. Louis Superintendency (still headed by William Clark) to trade with the Cheyennes, Arapahos, Kiowas, Snakes, Sioux, and Arikaras.[42]

In the meantime William Bent had entered into the Indian alcohol trade, ostensibly to compete with the Mexican whiskey merchants who hoped to dominate the skin and robe trade with the plains Indians whose hunting grounds were bisected by the Santa Fe Trail. Bent insisted he was "strongly opposed" to making alcohol available to Indians because it "endangered the trader's life" and could bring an end to "legitimate business." But he apparently knew well that alcohol was an essential commodity in the Indian trade and

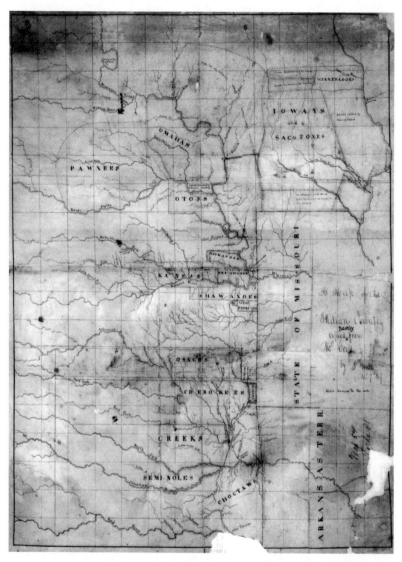

"Map of the [proposed] Indian Country 'partly' Copied from [Isaac] McCoy's [1832 map] by I. West, 7th Infantry," Map 54, Central Map Files, Cartographic Branch, National Archives and Records Administration.

therefore deployed a distribution strategy designed to lessen the dangers involved. After visits by village chiefs to Fort Bent, where orders for the illicit commodity were taken, said Bent, a company trader deposited kegs of liquor at the lodge of the principal chief and then:

> The Indians then came to the lodge and offered what they had to trade, and was assigned a keg of a certain size. . . . Each Indian then tied a piece of cloth or a string to mark it as his, and it was left in the chief's lodge, unopened, for the present. When the trade had been completed the trader left the village, and not until he had gone some distance did the chief permit the Indians to take their kegs of liquor and open them.[43]

Hundreds of miles east, in the more "habitable" area of Indian country, equally aggressive liquor merchants dispensed alcohol to Indians at will, even in the presence of federal agents. It was painful to observe, said Father Pierre-Jean DeSmet, from Bellevue, near the mouth of the Des Moines River, in the summer of 1839, that "wagon loads of the abominable stuff arrive daily from the settlements and along with it the very dregs of our white neighbors."[44]

Meanwhile, in far-off Washington, Secretary Cass busied himself with dividing the land west of Missouri for the anticipated wave of emigration to the new Indian country. To the agent for Indian affairs in Indiana, for example, Cass wrote:

> Some of the Indiana Delegation in Congress have expressed a wish that another effort be made to procure a cession of the Miami and Potawatomi reservations in that State. The President is willing to do this but in such manner as will avoid all expense to the United States. Believing that the object will be

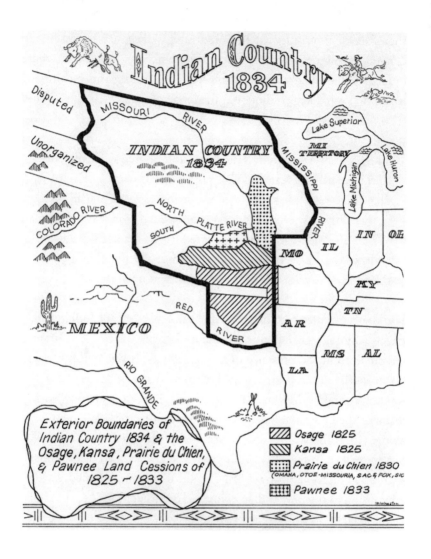

Indian Country 1834

INDIAN COUNTRY 1834

Disputed

Unorganized

MISSOURI RIVER

COLORADO RIVER

NORTH PLATTE RIVER

SOUTH

MEXICO

RED RIVER

RIO GRANDE

MISSISSIPPI RIVER

Lake Superior

MI TERRITORY

Lake Michigan

Lake Huron

IN OH

IL

MO

KY

TN

AR

LA

MS AL

Exterior Boundaries of
Indian Country 1834 & the
Osage, Kansa, Prairie du Chien,
& Pawnee Land Cessions of
1825 ~ 1833

Osage 1825

Kansa 1825

Prairie du Chien 1830
(OMAHA, OTOE-MISSOURIA, SAC & FOX, SIC

Pawnee 1833

better attained by entrusting it to a single individual without the usual expensive preparations of a treaty. You are therefore authorized at such times as you may find most convenient to open the subject to the Miamies and Potawatomies and explain to them the wish of the Government to purchase their reservations and to remove them to the Country West of the Mississippi. Enclosed you will find a map of the Western region approximated for the emigrating Indians. This communication you will consider confidential until, it becomes necessary for you to disclose the same to the Indians.[45]

Within months, for the sum of $250,000 and a few land grants to selected members of the tribe, Indian Agent William Marshall secured most of the land sought by the government. Six years later, on November 28, 1840, the Miamis ceded their remaining lands along the Wabash River and agreed to remove to an Indian country tract south of the Kansas River.[46] Although no occasion for celebration, it seemed the most reasonable course of action to tribal leaders, particularly when they recalled the words of a government commission to the Miamis ten years earlier: "If you continue where you now are [in Indiana] . . . and let the white people feed you whiskey and bring you bad habits, in a little while where will be the Miami Nation? They will all be swept off."[47]

Space was surely becoming place in the new Indian Country.

5

Presence

Given a consensus in the Indian Office that the new Indian country was no inhospitable wilderness but a place amenable to settlement and human progress, it was important to have reliable data regarding the number and character of the native people living in the region selected for the emigrant Indians' new homes in the West. Fortunately, the Reverend Jedidiah Morse, a popular and respected geographer of that time, accepted the War Department's invitation to prepare a scholarly overview of the American Indian population, including specific tribal numbers for the various regions of the United States. Not surprisingly, one of the regions selected by Morse for inclusion in his 1820 report to the government was "between the Missouri and Arkansas rivers & between the Mississippi and Rocky Mountains," a region that encompassed virtually all Indian country as defined by Congress in the Indian Trade and Intercourse Act of 1834. Happily for the architects of the new removal program, Morse counted only 101,072 natives in an area equal in size to nearly all of the United States east of the Appalachians.[1]

Not all of Morse's data were based on observations in the field, as was implied in the title of his report to the Secretary of War. Nor was Morse the first to attempt a count of Indians native to the region west of the Missouri. What Morse did was to reproduce or summarize selected population data compiled by explorers, travelers, government agents, traders, and missionaries dating back to the early 1800s and then to supplement this data with counts or estimates of his own, some based more on hearsay than fact. George M. Sibley's count of 1,600 Kansa Indians in 1816, for example, was reasonably close to the 1,465 members of the same tribe reported by Zebulon Pike a decade earlier and the 1,750 Kansa individuals counted by Indian Agent Richard W. Cummins in 1839. Collectively, the Sibley-Pike-Cummins data suggest that Morse's 1,800+ number for the Kansas was thus not far in excess of field counts done before and after 1820, thus pointing to the veracity of at least some parts of his report.[2] However, to claim that 10,000 "Arraphays" ranged on the headwaters of the Kansas River in 1820, as Morse did, was questionable at best.[3] Apart from the inaccuracy of at least some of his data, Morse's report provided much useful information. It was written in an engaging and nontechnical style, and it established quite clearly for the benefit of government officials and the public alike that a considerable number of native people hunted, traded, farmed, raised families, and actually *resided* in a region then being considered for tribal relocation: the semisedentary Dhegiha-Siouan Osages, Kansas, Omahas, Poncas, and Otoe-Missourias west and northwest of the present Omaha and Kansas City; the Caddoan Pawnee farmers and hunters in the middle Platte and Republican valleys; the numerous and diverse Lakota people living from gathering and wild game of the northern plains west of the Missouri River; the Cheyenne and Arapaho hunter-traders in the upper Arkansas River valley and along the eastern slope of the Continental Divide; and the highly mobile Kiowa and Comanche bison hunters ranging south of the Arkansas down into the panhandle country of present-day western Oklahoma and Texas.

In a letter to Governor William Clark less than a year prior to the Morse report to the government, Fort Osage Factor George C. Sibley had provided important information regarding tribal landownership west of the Missouri, as well as a timely and judicious means of obtaining that land for the benefit of the emigrant tribes. Based on wide travel in the new Indian country, supplemented by talks with tribal dignitaries who had come to trade at Fort Osage since 1808, Sibley observed:

> The Claims of our Indian Tribes to lands are so extremely vague and undefined, so conflicting and intermixed; that I cannot conceive a much more difficult task than to assign to each Tribe its proper limits—Therefore I think it would much better comport with the liberal views and benevolent policy of our government toward those poor creatures, to satisfy them all by annuities, in proportion to their numbers, for such lands as we desire to add to our domain. . . . Perhaps it would be just to say, that the forest and wilds of the Missouri belong in common to those Nations of Indians who live contiguous to them and Hunt thro' them. And that when our Govt thinks proper to reclaim those wilds for the use of our People, remuneration ought to be made in common to those Tribes whose natural pursuits are thus interfered with—Thus we should do justice to all, and satisfy all; which you know is the precise object of Govt; and which I am very certain can never be attained in any other manner.[4]

Complementing the Morse and Sibley reports was a map drawn by René Paul in 1816, entitled "A Map Exhibiting the Territorial limits of several Nations & Tribes of Indians agreeable to the Notes of A. Chouteau."[5] Paul was an accomplished St. Louis surveyor and son-in-law of Auguste Chouteau, whose notes were credited on

Paul's map as the source for his drawings. Chouteau was a prominent St. Louis businessman and civic leader, as was his brother Pierre, whom Secretary of War Henry Dearborn had commissioned first U.S. Indian Agent for the Upper Louisiana tribes in 1804. The Chouteau brothers had been involved in the western fur trade since the eighteenth century. Both had traveled extensively in the new Indian country and enjoyed a network of contacts with the tribes there with which they traded, and Auguste was generally recognized in and around the St. Louis area as an authority on Indian history, geography, and related land matters in the trans-Missouri West. All things considered, Auguste Chouteau was as knowledgeable about the location and extent of the Indian nations in the new Indian country as anyone, including Indian Office personnel in St. Louis and Washington.[6]

Paul made it be known that, excluding a small portion of present-day southeastern Missouri and northern Arkansas, the Foxes, Little Osages, Grand Osages, Kansez (Kansas), Missourias, Otoes, Iowas, Mahas (Omahas), Pawnees, and Sioux (Lakotas) claimed as their own all the land west of the Mississippi River to approximately the ninety-eighth meridian, and in the case of the Grand Osages, Pawnees, and Omahas, an undesignated distance beyond that line. There were no intervening areas or corridors between the "limits" of the several nations displayed on Paul's map, which indicated also that in terms of acreage and strategic location, the Osage, Kansa, and Fox nations presented the most significant obstruction to the relocation of Indians from the East.[7] Most of these Indians, who may have numbered well in the tens of thousands by the early 1830s, were familiar with, solicitous of, or addicted to the white man's weapons, alcohol, tools, food, and means of transit as a result of socioeconomic interaction with a considerable number of explorers, fugitives, traders, bootleggers, government officials, military personnel, and leisure travelers who had passed through their country since the turn

of the century—some by way of the increasingly popular and strategically positioned road connecting western Missouri and present-
day north-central New Mexico.

In the spring of 1827, for example, the line of march on the road to
Santa Fe was "at least a mile long" and composed of no fewer than
fifty-three wagons and several "pleasure" carriages; later that same
season, sixty traders with "a considerable amount of money" and 800
head of Mexican livestock worth $28,000 arrived in Missouri from
Santa Fe.[8] The value of this commerce increased year by year, and if
this commercial artery were in fact a persistently dangerous place requiring regular military patrols,[9] as politicians in Missouri and
Washington contended, the serious student of Indian country needs
to reflect on the peaceful, indeed cordial, meeting of supposed un-
trustworthy diplomatic rivals and savage Indians on the banks of the
Arkansas River 400 miles west of Missouri, in the late summer of
1829. About 200 men of the U.S. Sixth Infantry, commanded by Major Bennett Riley, were confronted by a company of 200 Mexican
regulars under the command of Colonel Jose Antonio Viscarra, ac-
companied by a diverse sampling of "Frenchmen, Creoles, and Mex-
icans," plus an undisclosed number of "polished gentlemen in
magnificent Spanish costume" and a somewhat less jubilant detach-
ment of Spaniards on their way to exile in the United States; a considerable amount of property in Mexican commodities and gold
consigned to the Missouri markets; members of several unidentified
Indian tribes but presumably Kiowas and/or Comanches residing in
that area; and no fewer than "2,000 horses, mules, [and] jacks." Following blithesome and long-winded welcomes on all sides, complemented by a formal dress review presented by both the U.S. and the
Mexican detachments, an evening meal of bread, salt pork, buffalo
meat, raw onions, and whiskey was served on a green blanket by
Major Riley and his men on August 11. The following evening
Colonel Viscarra and his aides responded in kind with a meal in a

large, decorative tent erected on the banks of the Arkansas. Presented on a long, low table complemented by furniture decorated in "pure silver," the meal included fried ham, a variety of cakes, "delightful" chocolate, and several wines "direct from Santa Fe." Several languages were spoken at the various events, prompting Lieutenant Philip St. George Cooke of the American garrison to report that it was "the strangest collection of men and animals that had perhaps ever met on a frontier of the United States."[10]

And it may well have been. But at the level of incipient Manifest Destiny and especially American designs on Oregon and California, the Riley-Viscarra meeting of 1829 was a graphic example that no area of the contemplated Indian country was secure from outside incursions, not even from those with nonbelligerent intent. Other overland roads, some extending to the Pacific coast itself, were as much in the national interest as an enlightened removal policy, asserted a prominent eastern newspaper in 1818. Indeed, it was no idle dream to suggest that "within a few years we may hear of a national road winding through the passes of the Rocky mountains . . . between the city of New York and a great city built at the mouth of the Columbia."[11]

Only a few months prior to the Riley-Viscarra meeting, William L. Sublette and a company of fifty-two men and two Indians had left St. Louis for the annual fur-trade rendezvous at Pierre's Hole, in what is now eastern Idaho. Their initial route took them down the Santa Fe road only recently marked by Sibley and his crew. West of present-day Topeka they forded the Kansas River and headed northwest to the Little Blue, and then to the Platte, a route soon to be know as "Sublette's Trace," or the eastern leg of the Oregon-California Trail, eventually traveled by thousands of white emigrants seeking a better life in the Far West.[12]

In the spring of 1831 John Gantt and Jefferson Blackwell took seventy mounted trappers up the Kansas-Blue-Platte route to the

Laramie Mountains, and a few months later, Captain Benjamin L. E. Bonneville, on leave from army duties to pursue his own commercial interests but on a mission also that "encompassed a good deal more than commerce," followed the same route. In St. Louis the War Department had given Bonneville detailed instructions for exploring future Indian country west to the Rocky Mountains, and even beyond, with the view of carrying on trade with the Indians and determining "the quality of the soil, productions, the minerals, the natural history, the climate, the Geography and Topography, as well as the Geology of various parts of the Country . . . belonging to the United States between our frontier, and the Pacific." In short, Bonneville "was to serve the cause of national expansion" but not in an official capacity.[13] Others soon followed and in much greater numbers, not the least of which was the Bidwell-Bartleson party of sixty individuals (including five women and perhaps up to ten children) that traveled from Independence to California in 1841,[14] thus demonstrating that the Indian country west of Missouri was no obstacle to the wonders of the American West.

The white man's presence west of the Missouri was felt in other and more deadly ways. In midsummer 1831, smallpox broke out among the emigrant Shawnees only a few miles west of Missouri, and by early fall it was reported that at least a dozen had died and that the disease was "raging among the different tribes and the Indians were flying in different directions" to escape the vicious malady.[15] Unlike Sublette, Bonneville, and the Bidwell-Bartleson party, most of the Indians then living in the trans-Missouri West had had little or no previous contact with the dreaded disease and were, therefore, as an important study of "virgin soil" epidemics among native Americans has emphasized, "immunological[ly] almost defenseless."[16] To its credit, Congress responded with the law of May 5, 1832, providing for "extending the benefits of [smallpox] vaccination to Indians and to thus save them from the destructive ravages of the disease."[17] But for most natives of the trans-Missouri West it was too late. By 1827 Superintendent William Clark had reported that 180 Kansas were dead of smallpox;[18] from there the disease spread to the Shawnees, then northwest to the Otoe-Missourias, the Omahas and Poncas, and finally to the Pawnees in the Loup Valley 80 miles above the mouth of the Platte. The catastrophic details are best recounted in the words of Indian Agent John Dougherty, who wrote from Cantonment Leavenworth on October 29, 1831:

> I have returned from a visit to four Pawnee villages, all of whom I found in a most deplorable condition. Indeed, their misery defies all description. Judging from what I saw during the four days I spent with them, and the information I received from the chiefs and two Frenchmen who reside with them . . . I am fully persuaded that one half the whole number of souls of each village have and will be carried off by this cruel and frightful distemper. They told me that not one under 33 years of age escaped the monstrous disease. . . . They were dying so fast, and taken down at once in such large numbers that they had ceased to bury their dead. . . . Their misery was so great and so general, that they seemed to be unconscious of it, and to look upon the dead and dying as they would so many dead horses.[19]

How many Indians actually died in the epidemic of 1827–1831 is not known, but surely it was in the thousands. In addition to the 180 Kansa deaths reported by Clark, Dr. Johnston Lykins stated in 1832, based on information from Agent Dougherty, that more than 4,000 Otoe-Missourias, Omahas, Poncas, and Pawnees had perished in 1831 alone, and that of that number more than 3,000 were Pawnees.[20]

Even so, fatalities in such numbers and the socioeconomic chaos that followed did not prompt the government to alter its plan for a buffer zone at the Platte River that would protect the emigrant Indians from unfriendly tribes to the north, that is, the Pawnees and Lakotas. Therefore, in the fall of 1833, U.S. Commissioner Henry L. Ellsworth was dispatched to the mouth of the Platte, where he was able to secure a cession from the Otoe-Missourias for all their land between the Little and Big Nemahaw rivers south of the Platte, one of the most attractive areas for agriculture (and land speculation) west of the Missouri. He then headed west to the main Pawnee village, where survivors of the recent smallpox epidemic were reported wandering about "like persons who [had] passed through a burning prairie." At this juncture the most reasonable and humane action might have been to pay the Pawnees outright for the right of transit over a well-defined route, like the Santa Fe Trail agreement with the Kansa tribe eight years earlier. This payment alone, however, would provide no new land for tribal relocation. Under the direction of Commissioner Ellsworth, therefore, the Grand, Republican, Loup, and Tape Pawnees were persuaded to cede all their Nebraska land south of the Platte and south into the upper Solomon Valley of present-day northwestern Kansas as well, for twelve annual payments of $4,600 in goods "not exceeding St. Louis prices," and $33,500 for teaching the Pawnees how to farm and educate their children. All this was negotiated, it should be noted, while the Senate was authorizing trade licenses and passports for non-Indians to enter Indian country and at the same time requiring, by Article 9 of the 1833 treaty, that the Pawnees "not molest or injure the person or property of *any white citizen of the United States, wherever found*" (emphasis added).[21]

Agreement to such terms was one thing, but enforcement was another. Like the Osages and Kansas to the south and the Lakotas to the north, the Pawnees were not unaware that the overland caravans were depleting their bison and antelope herds and that the invaders were overgrazing the prairie-plains and harvesting the limited amount of timber available west of the Missouri. The Pawnees therefore retaliated by demanding tribute from the overland travelers under the belief that their actions did not violate Article 9 of the 1833 treaty, which provided for tribute in the form of specie and provisions from the passing trains when government agents certified that the overlanders had the right to travel over the Pawnee hinterland. One such traveler, for example, reported from the Platte road that the men of her caravan refused to pay simply because they were certain that "the country they were traveling across belonged to the United States." So persistent were arguments over the Indian tribute business that by 1848 Indian Superintendent Thomas H. Harvey predicted violence if remedial action were not taken. The purchase of an explicit right-of-way through the whole of Indian country was Harvey's unequivocal recommendation.[22]

His counsel was ignored, most likely because Secretary of War Lewis Cass in the meantime had determined that

> Indians committing depredations, generally do this secretly . . . where there are no witnesses. Cattle and hogs are killed and horses stolen, and these are the most usual depredations. They are committed when there is no one by to witness or report the transaction. . . . It is obvious therefore that if the same proof is necessary to produce pecuniary compensation for these injuries as would be to convict and punish the parties, then the provisions of the intercourse act become totally inoperative and the object of the law, which was to preserve peace on the frontiers by preventing retaliation for injuries would fail of attainment.[23]

Having consulted with the attorney general of the United States, Cass ruled that a simple sworn statement by a white claimant against an Indian would henceforth constitute "proper testimony to be received in the examination of depredation claims."[24] Such heavy-handed action was, of course, welcomed by the overlanders as much as it was resented by the Indians, particularly when it is remembered that theft, not murder or other less severe acts of violence, were the principal complaints of white travelers on the road to Oregon and California.[25] Indeed, the circumstances under which Cass saw fit to assert his authority in the 1830s were not unlike Chief Little Robe's description of the Cheyennes' dilemma on the southern plains several decades later: "Your people make big talk and sometimes make war, if an Indian kills a white man's ox to keep his wife and children from starving; what do you think my people ought to say when they see their [buffalo] killed by your race when you are not hungry?"[26]

In the larger picture, however, it was the mere possibility of gaining access to acres and acres of fertile land west of Missouri and Iowa that boded well for a non-Indian presence there in the future. In 1831, based on personal observation, Isaac McCoy flatly asserted that the soil for more than 200 miles west of Missouri was "almost universally rich" and could be "safely considered favorable to settlement";[27] four years later, after a summer expedition through Indian country, Colonel Henry Dodge endorsed McCoy's assessment.[28] An even more comprehensive and certainly more public pronouncement of settlement possibilities beyond the Missouri came from the pen of Matthew C. Field, who traveled from St. Louis to South Pass with Sir William Drummond Stewart's party in 1843.

Field was an assistant editor of the New Orleans *Daily Picayune* and well-known for his poems and feature stories over the signature "Phazama." He had traveled to Santa Fe in 1839, mainly for health reasons but also to learn more about the upper Arkansas country and thus was no novice regarding the flora, fauna, and topographical features of one particular area of Indian country. His 1843 route was up the Kansas River to the mouth of the Little Blue and then on the Platte route taken by the Bidwell-Bartleson party two years earlier. In a *Picayune* article, "The Country about the Kansas," dated January 6, 1844, Field went out of his way to extol the potential of the country directly west of Missouri, particularly for agriculture. On the question of who was leading the way in this regard, his words are worth quoting in some detail:

> By far the most promising region, in an agricultural point of view, that we passed over in our whole route, was that along the banks and in the vicinity of the Kansas river. We saw no other land as good during our further progress West, but, on the contrary, traveled over soil every way inferior, and lacking advantages necessary for the farmer. The Willamette or Wallamette Valley in Oregon is the first favorable locality for farming purposes that is met after leaving Kansas. . . . The Kansas is belted by a noble growth of timber, and a number of farms lie snugly ensconced within the shelter of the forest. Some of these are owned and occupied by intelligent half-breeds, or by French traders who have gained the land through Government provision, by marrying educated women of the Kansas nation.[29]

Such public confirmation of the attractiveness of the area west of Missouri may have been cause for celebration among the Shawnees, Delawares, Wyandots, Potawatomis, Kickapoos, Ottawas, and Sacs and Foxes who only a few years earlier had agreed to move there under the government's removal policy. But Field's intelligence to the effect that Indian land could be secured through "Government provision" was surely of interest to other traders, as well as to struggling farmers trying to eke out a living during the difficult times following the Panic of 1837.[30]

Gaining land through "Government provision" was an obvious reference to Article 6 of the Kansa land cession treaty of June 3, 1825, which granted a reservation "one mile square" on the north bank of the Kansas River, beginning near present-day Topeka and "extending down the Kanzas river for quantity," to each of the twenty-three "half-breeds" of the Kansa nation.[31] Superintendent Clark, as we have seen,[32] justified the granting of these individual reservations on the grounds that separate property and a fixed residence in the hands of these individuals would promote civilization among the less fortunate full-blood members of the tribe and, perhaps, among other tribes as well.

Neither of these supposed cultural virtues, however, dealt with the underlying objective of the individual grants, that is, enlisting the aid of Kansa Chief Nompawarah (The White Plume) in persuading the other Kansa leaders and warriors to join with him in ceding millions of acres of land to the government. Not unlike similar provisions in other Indian treaties that reportedly were "negotiated" during the removal era, these fee-simple grants (that is, grants with no restrictions on transfer of ownership to non-Indians) were the bedrock of a virtually no-cost strategy that by 1846 had divested the Kansa nation of 23,168,640 acres of land,[33] nearly half of the present state of Kansas. But how was it that Nompawarah so easily succumbed to the overtures of Superintendent Clark in the first place?

To his credit, Nompawarah obtained $70,000 in annuities for his people (to be distributed in $3,500 payments over a twenty-year period), as well as sundry farm tools, livestock, a farm instructor, and the promise of educational assistance for the children of his tribe. But Clark's trump cards, of course, were the twenty-three "half-breed" grants, five of which went to Chief Nompawarah's grandchildren and another to the daughter of the official tribal interpreter, Baptis Ducherut, who was himself related to several of the other grantees. Apart from the possibility of alienating the grants, which was legally confirmed in 1862,[34] Clark's contention that by residing on and personally cultivating their property, the "half-breeds" would enjoy a civilizing influence over the Kansa full-bloods was at best misguided and at worst blatantly impossible. Insisting that one family could physically operate a 640-acre farm with the technology of that time flew in the face of the government's own contention nearly four decades later that one quarter section of land (160 acres) was the ideal size for a sustainable and productive family farm.

It is important to note that all of the Kansa "half-breeds" were minors in 1825. Several were living with relatives in St. Louis or near the mouth of the Kansas River, and none were then able to understand how it was that for having been awarded an individual plot of land the government expected them to play an active role in the "civilization" of their fellow tribesmen. In fact none of them even occupied their tracts prior to 1840, which by then were so embroiled in legal disputes and survey problems with the emigrant Delawares that their value, as proclaimed by Superintendent Clark only three years earlier, was open to dispute.[35]

A similar but perhaps more creative variation of the land-grant strategy for opening up land west of Missouri was to grant individual plots (what came to be designated land "floats") to individual Indians with no designated location other than that they be selected in Indian country as defined by the law of 1834. Article 14 of the Wyandot removal treaty of 1842, for example, provided that thirty-five members of the Wyandot tribe designated "by blood or adoption" be awarded 640 acres (or a total of 22,400 acres) to be located "on any lands west of the Missouri River set apart for Indian use, not already claimed or occupied by any person or tribe."[36] The result was that more than 22,000 acres of Indian country land were placed on the market for non-Indians to develop, land that in part became the Kansas town sites of Lecompton, Doniphan, Emporia, Topeka, Lawrence, Burlington, Manhattan, and Kansas City. Once the inclusion of individual Indian land grants on the model of the Wyandot treaty of 1842 was accepted by Indian Office officials, it was difficult if not impossible to secure concessions from tribal leaders without them.[37] This certainly was the case with the Kansa and Wyandot grants, suggesting that the demand for fee-simple title to land in Indian country was urged on by the government's own actions.[38]

But the most dramatic contravention of the government's "strong fence" policy came almost before the ink was dry on the Indian country law of 1834. In question was the northwest corner of Missouri encompassing more than 3,000 square miles of today's Holt, Buchanan, Andrew, Nodaway, Atchison, and Platte counties. Why this fertile, well-timbered, and strategically positioned tract west of a straight line due north from the mouth of the Kansas River to the present-day Missouri-Iowa border was not included in the original Missouri statehood bill is uncertain, although Missouri Senator Lewis F. Linn contended in 1835 that "a critical knowledge of the geography was not to be obtained, or this piece of land would not, it is reasonable to suppose, have been left out of our [state] limits."[39]

Representative Horace Everett of the House Committee on Indian Affairs, however, insisted that when Missouri was admitted to the union in 1820, "it was supposed that new states would be created out of adjoining territories and as a matter of course a longitudinal line was adopted."[40] Certainly the area in question was considered extremely desirable terrain by both the Indians (principally the Sacs and Foxes, Ioways, and Otoe-Missourias) and the white population of western Missouri. Responding to a request from Senator Linn for information regarding the "propriety or impropriety of attaching to the State of Missouri a strip of territory lying between her western borders and the Missouri river," former Ioway subagent John L. Bean and Indian trader Pierre Menard reported on February 6, 1835, more than half a year *after* Indian country had been established by law, that "the location of any Indian tribe on this country (could any be got to accept it) would be the fruitful source of strife and difficulties."[41] On his part (and in line with the Bean-Menard report) Senator Linn advised Secretary Cass that "allured by its various advantages" and confident that the federal government would see fit to detach this modest section of land from Indian country and make it a part of Missouri, many white families had already established farms there and were confident that the recently imposed Indian removal policy would not add more to the "accumulated horde upon horde along our borders, ready and willing at any favorable moment to rush our frontier settlements," and he insisted that "Congress, by giving it [the land in question] to Missouri, will only be doing *now* what should have been done at first."[42] The ball was now in the hands of Cass.

As early as 1825, Thomas L. McKenney, chief clerk in the War Department's Office of Indian Affairs, had described Cass as "the best informed man in the United States on Indian affairs."[43] But he claimed ignorance regarding the "modest section of land" Senator Linn and his constituents hoped to detach from Indian country and hand over to Missouri. Responding to Senator Linn's letter, Secretary Cass wrote:

> I must confess I was not aware that stipulations of the treaty of Prairie du Chien of 1830, affected the tenure of country lying between the State of Missouri and the Missouri river, until my attention was called to the matter. The subject seems placed beyond the reach of this Department, till Congress shall be pleased to act in relation to it. In the meantime, however, no arrangement will be entered into for the removal of any Indian tribes to that district of [Indian] country, till Congress shall have an opportunity of finally settling the question presented by you.[44]

In the Prairie du Chien negotiations, involving leaders of northern Sioux bands and representatives of the Sac and Fox, Ioway, Otoe, Missouria, and Omaha tribes, Indian Superintendent William Clark's response to the Indians' demand for more compensation than the government was prepared to offer was to remind them that "the Country we want to purchase is in fact an Indian Country" by law and that the land could be assigned and/or allotted "to the Tribes now living thereon, *or to such other Tribes as the President may locate thereon for hunting, and other purposes*" (emphasis added).[45]

Under authority of the Indian Removal Act of 1830 the government was, of course, eager to put the ceded area to use, and in the fall of 1833, certain bands of the Ottawa, Chippewa, and Potawatomi tribes agreed by treaty to relinquish their claims to parts of northeastern Illinois, southeastern Wisconsin, and southern Michigan for cash and other considerations, including new lands on a 5,000,000-acre Indian country tract in what is now southwestern Iowa and northwestern Missouri.[46] As subsequently determined by federal officials, most of the Potawatomi assignment was in the contested area sought by Missouri officials and the white squatters already resident there. What followed was a confrontation between the Potawatomis and the federal government, ceaselessly urged on by the Missourians, with the outcome never really in doubt. On March 28, 1837, President Martin Van Buren declared that all Indian titles to the "fertile triangle" of northwestern Missouri had been extinguished, thus effectuating immediately the act of Congress of June 7, 1836, allowing for the extension of Missouri's northern boundary. When this news reached the border country, "a general season of celebration ensued" among the white people there. According to one contemporary account, "bonfires were lighted, speeches were made, barrel heads were hammered in and merrily the flowing bowl went around" in the fledgling non-Indian settlements directly north of present-day Kansas City.[47]

Meanwhile, the now-designated "Missouri" Potawatomis were forced to seek cover behind a new government fence, this time on a reservation in the more remote Marais des Cygnes Valley of today's eastern Kansas, 100 miles to the southwest.[48] Truly, the white man's presence was becoming manifest in the new Indian country.

6

Proscription

The new Indian country as understood by its creators was a practical solution to the young America's recurring problem of space for unwanted Indians. Space in this sense, however, was not only rivers, valleys, mountains, plains, flora and fauna, or particular sections of terrain set off by surveyors to indicate where the Indians ought to be. Rather, as suggested at the onset of this study, it was an inducement that first had to be imagined and then created. In short, to have meaning, space required fashioning it into a purposeful place.[1] At the imaginative level this creation involved gift giving and speech making designed to persuade the Indians of the government's paternalistic concern (that is, authority) and good intentions, followed by more substantive (and often manipulative) talks culminating in written documents signed by government officials and tribal leaders of supposed equal diplomatic standing, calling for the Indians' removal to the promised land. The more creative step, in contrast, called for a variety of prescriptive remedies for social, economic, and moral improvement, as well as proscriptive standards for the Indians' behavior once they were well established within the protective confines of the new Canaan.

The prescriptive realm was varied in terms of individual and tribal needs, including annuities, livestock, wagons, seeds, farm tools, grist mills, sawmills, wagons, blacksmiths, schools, teachers, housing, clothing, daily rations, general merchandise, fee-simple land grants to selected tribal members, payment of tribal debts, and the services of a government agent or subagent employed to look after the Indians' best interests. Most prescriptions were spelled out in treaties principally generated by executive officials and the Indians themselves (and ratified by the Senate),[2] whereas the bulk of the proscriptive code was conceived by legislative committees and commissions and written into generally less permissive laws by Congress. Thus it was that the 1834 law "to regulate trade and intercourse with the Indian tribes and to preserve peace on the frontiers" contained proscriptions for licensing traders and other non-Indians desiring admission into Indian country; for trading or bartering with Indians; for driving and disposing of livestock in Indian country; for expelling intruders from Indian country; for the character of military authority in Indian country; for purchasing or leasing land from Indians in Indian country; for speaking about Indian treaties resulting in the excitement of war against the United States in Indian country; for encouraging or enticing foreign countries to war against Indian nations or individuals in Indian country; for stealing or destroying property in Indian country; for crimes and federal judicial authority in Indian country; and especially for prohibiting the sale or barter of alcohol and the operation of distilleries in Indian country.[3]

Although the 1834 law therefore allowed the federal government to take on the role of the Indians' protector in general, it was proscriptive also for those particular Indians who might consume or in any way become involved with alcohol under the statute of July 9, 1832, which held that "no ardent spirits shall be hereafter introduced, under any pretense, into the Indian country."[4] In effect, then, the

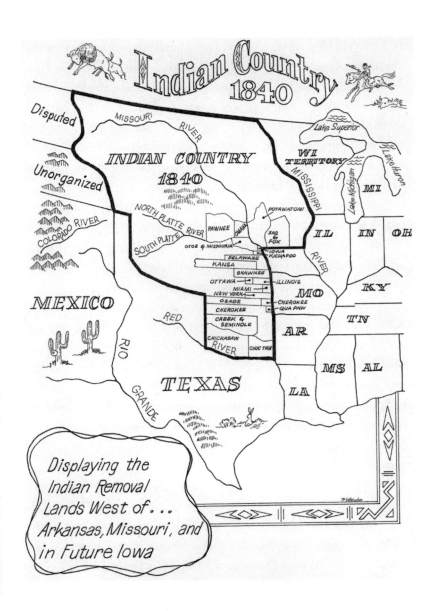

Indian Country 1840

Disputed

MISSOURI RIVER

Lake Superior

INDIAN COUNTRY 1840

WI TERRITORY

Unorganized

MISSISSIPPI

Lake Michigan

Lake Huron

MI

COLORADO RIVER

NORTH PLATTE RIVER

SOUTH PLATTE

PAWNEE

OMAHA

POTAWATOMI

SAC & FOX

IL

IN

OH

OTOE & MISSOURIA

IOWA
KICKAPOO

DELAWARE

KANSA

SHAWNEE

OTTAWA

MIAMI

ILLINOIS

MEXICO

NEW YORK

OSAGE

CHEROKEE

QUA PAW

MO

KY

RIVER

CHEROKEE

CREEK &
SEMINOLE

RED

CHICKASAW

RIVER

CHOCTAW

AR

TN

RIO GRANDE

TEXAS

LA

MS

AL

Displaying the
Indian Removal
Lands West of...
Arkansas, Missouri, and
in Future Iowa

1832 and 1834 laws taken together constituted a powerful tool for the fine-tuning of a practice dating back to 1643, when officials in New Netherland prohibited "all Tapsters and other Inhabitants" from "selling directly or indirectly any liquors to Indians."[5] But the substantial profits to be had from selling rum to Indians and the myriad problems of enforcement, not only in New Netherland but also in other areas of colonial America, suggested that the prevention or even moderation of Indian drinking by law was generally ineffective;[6] nevertheless, the United States opted for the regulation and control of alcohol for Indians almost from the start.[7]

In the first Jefferson administration, for example, a proviso was attached to the Indian Trade and Intercourse Act of 1802 empowering the executive branch to "prevent or restrain [as it saw fit] the vending or distribution of spirituous liquors among all or any of the said Indian tribes."[8] This was followed by an 1815 law prohibiting the operation of distilleries in Indian country.[9] But because the legal boundaries of Indian country could be abruptly altered by any Indian treaty involving the cession of land or a change in tribal landownership, and since alcohol in concentrated form could be transported from the point of manufacture with minimum difficulty (and certainly without fear of spoilage!), the law of 1815 was of little value in halting the flow of alcohol to Indians, even to those residing in the upper Missouri River country, where in 1820, with no apparent difficulty, the Missouri Fur Company shipped 800 gallons of St. Louis whiskey to its Indian trading camps.[10]

The response to violations of the 1815 and 1802 laws was an amendment to the intercourse act of 1802, empowering the War Department and interested citizens to seek out and seize any and all "ardent spirits" in Indian country. Passed into law only a few days after the factory system of regulation was terminated by Congress in favor of returning to open competition in the Indian trade, the new alcohol law of May 6, 1822, provided that the mere "suspicion or information" regarding the possession of alcohol was adequate cause for instigating alcohol searches in Indian country. One half of the alcohol seized went to the informant and the other half to the government. Bonds of licensed Indian traders alleged to have been involved in the illegal transaction could be placed into legal suit by the government.[11] Yet precisely *where* this latest proscription should be applied and enforced remained unclear.

In Michigan Territory, perhaps? Colonel Joshua Snelling was so inclined, not long after the 1822 law went into effect. In a letter to the secretary of war he wrote: "I have taken a house about three miles from town [Detroit] and passing from it I had daily opportunities of seeing the road literally strewed with the bodies of [Indian] men, women, and children in the last stages of brutal intoxication. . . . I was informed by a person of veracity that one man (a Mr. _____) has purchased this season above three hundred blankets for whiskey; these cost him, on the average, about seventy-five cents each."[12] Snelling acknowledged that alcohol was readily available from the British at nearby Malden—a routine complaint of most War Department officials at that time—but he insisted that the main source of supply for the Detroit whiskey traders was St. Louis, certainly well within the boundaries of the United States. But what Snelling failed to note was that as a result of the Chippewa, Wyandot, and Potawatomi land cession treaty of November 17, 1807,[13] the actual area where he had observed the Indians' "brutal intoxication" was no longer a part of Indian country, a not atypical example of the "where" problem of Indian country that William Clark and Lewis Cass in their 1829 report to Congress would term as too "tedious to describe."[14]

It was this sort of problem that prompted many of the removal Indians to voice serious concerns regarding their future in the trans-Missouri West. Only a few months after the stringent alcohol law of July 9, 1832, went into effect, a band of Kickapoos that in 1819 had ceded land in Illinois in exchange for land in southwestern Missouri was again called upon to move, this time to the area immediately west of Fort Leavenworth. There white squatters and their political supporters were calling for the blanket expulsion of all Indians and immediate annexation of the "fertile triangle" to the state of Missouri. While the Kickapoos were making preparations for the final move across the Missouri in the fall of 1833, a tribal delegation informed Connecticut Congressman E. A. Ellsworth, a staunch opponent of Indian removal,[15] that their people "were afraid of the wicked water brought us by our white friends" and that they wanted "to get out of its reach by land or water."[16] Ellsworth responded: "Your Great Father is going to help you. . . . The wicked water of which you speak has been carried two hundred miles further into the [Indian] country. Your Great Father was very sorry when the wicked water was brought into the [Indian] country; but he will stop it, and will punish the wicked men who brought it by Judges sent to try them."[17]

Two hundred miles west meant that the whiskey traders had already staked out most of the more desirable area for settling the removal Indians and that the Indian alcohol industry in western Missouri and Arkansas was sure to grow by leaps and bounds once the imaginary line separating Indian from non-Indian country became law in 1834. And contrary to Congressman Ellsworth's statement to the Kickapoos, the alcohol trade had already reached Bent's Fort and the Cheyenne-Arapaho country 500 miles west of Fort Leavenworth by 1830,[18] while hundreds of miles to the southeast, from Fort Smith and nearby Van Buren, Arkansas, bootleggers were increasing their illicit trade with the Cherokees. "It is doing the most horrid mischief," reported the *Missionary Herald.* "Men, women and children are daily to be seen and unavoidably heard in a state of brutal intoxication. . . . All this whiskey comes from white men residing out of the nation."[19]

An uncritical view suggests that the laws of 1832 and 1834 provided a means of lowering, if not eliminating, the destructive level of Indian drinking in the new Indian country. Yet these very same proscriptions provided no enforceable means of preventing any Indian residing in the Indian country from crossing back over the "strong fence" into the white settlements in Missouri for alcohol, in a manner not unlike what had been his or her experience in the East prior to removal. Such lack of foresight, if that is what it actually was, could therefore not be attributed to a lack of information regarding the manner in which Indians had obtained alcohol in the past. And, in fact, Lewis Cass himself had written in 1827 that the most extreme measure of Indian intoxication, one that in the course of human nature presented no comparable phenomenon, was among those Indians "in immediate contact with our settlements."[20]

The 1834 law did allow for a fine not to exceed $300 for any person transporting alcohol into the Indian country;[21] but then the problems of enforcement took over with telling effect. In a speech to the Stokes Commission soon after the 1834 law was enacted, a prominent Shawnee chief recounted some details of enforcement near the future site of Kansas City:

> We know whiskey is bad. But a few days ago, when our agent read to us his instructions from our great father, our young men went to Independence [Missouri] where they met some white traders in whiskey who said there was no law against Indians taking whiskey into their country, and nobody said so except their Agent and bad men at the Fort [Leavenworth]. The white men told our young men to take some whiskey even to Mr. [Agent] Cummins's house and they would not be punished. If the whites should put them into jail, they would go and let them out again. We are sorry my father that this is so—

we have no law and our great Father does not put into execution those he makes himself.[22]

A Delaware warrior confirmed what the Shawnee leader had said:

Whiskey is bad for our people. We see it every day, but the whites first gave us whiskey. . . . We cannot keep our young men from going into the states. The traders along the [Missouri] line have "a heap" of whiskey. Our men drink some and bring some home. We have no law and it is a difficult thing to stop. But we know it is a bad thing.[23]

Commissioner Henry Ellsworth, who was party to the Indians' testimony, in effect agreed by recounting the fortunes of three white persons apprehended in Indian country with two barrels of illicit whiskey in their possession and then brought to Independence for trial. With such an abundance of incriminating evidence, the defendants should have been summarily convicted, suggested Ellsworth, but because "the criminals were defended by able Counsellors, one a distinguished advocate from St. Louis,—all were acquitted."[24]

What characterized the alcohol question in Indian country during the next two decades was a dramatic increase in drinking along the Santa Fe Trail, which the whiskey traders continued to regard as a public right-of-way for transporting their commodities to local or distant places at will; or a place to consume, as only a few years earlier Major Riley's and Colonel Viscarra's troops had, all the ardent spirits they or their associates desired.[25] Moreover, it should be emphasized that Indians could obtain all the alcohol they could pay for at 110 Mile Crossing, southwest of the present Kansas City, at Council Grove, on the upper Neosho, at Lost Springs, at Cottonwood Crossing, and at Cow Creek Crossing, all on the Santa Fe Trail. Or in Cherokee and Choctaw country to the south, where the

Arkansas bootleggers provided their native customers with an ample supply of the illegal commodity. And especially along the Missouri River, from the mouth of the Kansas to the mouth of the Platte, where the Missouri distillers and alcohol vendors plied their trade directly across the legal boundary of Indian country with impunity. "Indians across the [Missouri] river drew annuities," recalled one early white settler with unabashed candor, "so that the trade was safe and almost without exception on a cash basis."[26]

There was a defect, therefore, in the government's design for interdicting the flow of alcohol in Indian country, a defect that surely was anticipated at some level by the architects and champions of removal policy. Even a cursory reading of the removal treaties suggests that most if not all contained unambiguous proscriptions for socioeconomic change and moral behavior as defined by the Indians' Great Father in Washington. A summary reading of these same treaties also shows that material awards were the rule, not the exception, and that these awards were principally in the form of undeveloped or underdeveloped realty whose value most certainly would appreciate with little or no effort on the Indians' part; or in the form of hard currency regularly issued over a period of several years or even decades, providing the Indians with significant buying power for the white man's merchandise.

In the year preceding passage of the removal bill of 1830, the total amount of money due to Indians was just under $250,000;[27] following removal, that figure increased dramatically. By the treaties of 1838 and 1840, for example, the Miamis alone were owed $885,000; the government's obligation by the treaty of 1833 with the Ottawas was $93,200, and by the treaty of 1832 with the Kickapoos, $113,000. Comparable amounts were awarded to the Delawares, Potawatomis, Wyandots, Shawnees, Sacs and Foxes, and several of the smaller Illinois tribes.[28] According to one estimate that included funds earmarked for the Five Civilized Tribes west of Arkansas, the grand total (including trust funds) had increased to nearly $30,000,000 by 1845,[29] and a fairly typical example of the actual amount of annuity income that went to the traders is that of the Confederated and Missouri Sac and Fox tribes, who under separate treaties negotiated in Washington on October 21, 1837, were owed $17,970 in annuity interest by the government but who were left with only $2,970 after their whiskey creditors had been paid off at their agency in Iowa. Since their return from the treaty table in Washington, reported the Sac and Fox agent that same year, "the whole of the two tribes have done little else than live upon their presents of horses &c. given them, drink whiskey, and live amongst the white settlers on their borders and in their country."[30]

Government indecision regarding the most equitable method of dispersing actual annuity dollars constituted another flaw in the proscriptive design. Prior to 1834, annuities were paid to individual Indians or their families on a pro rata basis, but after that date payments were made to chiefs or other respected tribal members, presumably because they were more trustworthy or, perhaps, endowed with special talents for making equitable distributions. But that was not the case. Alcohol consumption continued unabated, leading to a new federal law in 1847 that for the first time authorized prison sentences of up to two years for those convicted in a U. S. District Court of selling or even attempting to sell alcohol to Indians in Indian country. The law also granted discretionary authority to the executive branch for deciding whether annuities should once again be paid to heads of Indian families or to the tribe as a whole for their "happiness and prosperity."[31]

An initial flurry of optimism that the alcohol trade might thus be brought under control soon gave way to pessimism and open criticism of the 1847 law, and ultimately to Indian Commissioner William Medill's recommendation that all intoxicated Indians be arrested and placed in prison at hard labor. But the War Department took no action,[32] and in 1849 newly installed Indian Commissioner Orlando Brown flatly asserted that the federal legislation and the efforts of the military and civilian agents in the field had not lessened the amount of alcohol available or consumed by Indians in Indian country. Conceding that the "extent of the Indian frontier and the impossibility of guarding it at every point" in concert with the traders' callous, almost "fiend-like" disregard for the Indians were the primary factors underlying the deplorable situation, Brown went further by emphasizing that the traders continued to engage in the annuity-alcohol enterprise for the simple reason that the profits were "so enormous as to stimulate them to encounter a considerable risk in doing so."[33] And indeed they were. In 1831, for example, undiluted alcohol priced at $1 a gallon in St. Louis brought no less than $30 in Indian country. Three years later, the profit had more than tripled: $.25 per gallon in St. Louis to $25 per gallon west of Missouri and Arkansas. That same year also, alcohol distilled at the mouth of the Yellowstone, hundreds of miles up the Missouri River but still within the limits of Indian country, was priced at $64 a gallon.[34]

So much for trader profits, a matter surely not difficult to understand. Legal risks under the 1847 law, however, presented greater challenges for the traders—although not always threatening or generally unsurmountable for those charged with illicit sales and taken to court. On April 13, 1847, Secretary of War William L. Marcy issued a departmental directive regarding fines, imprisonment, destruction of distilleries, revocation of trade licenses, and the like under the new Indian alcohol law, and three months later one of the first cases under the directive was heard in a Missouri federal court: Abraham Potter's alleged sale of whiskey to Indians in Indian country. For reasons not recorded by the court, the case was continued to March 1853 and then to the following October, when it was continued again "because the defendant could not be found." Nine months later the case was dismissed on grounds that all the witnesses had simply disappeared. Penalties, moreover, often were of no great concern for convicted traders, as evidenced by the sentence of "one dollar cash" and confinement to prison for one hour handed out in 1848 to Samuel E. Roby by a federal court in Missouri for "swindling and selling brandy to the Ottawas."[35]

Indian agents in the field almost routinely complained that state laws intended to prohibit or regulate the Indian alcohol trade in Missouri, Arkansas, and Iowa—seeking to deny Indian country Indians yet another *place* to purchase and consume alcohol legally—were openly "disregarded and laughed at,"[36] and when similar laws were proposed for consideration by federal officials, they were dismissed on the grounds that the matter involved the issue of state sovereignty—certainly by then an increasingly divisive national issue. Even so, reported Commissioner Medill in 1848, the Indian alcohol problem would never be brought under control until the border states came forward with more stringent laws designed "to restrain the evil disposed among their citizens . . . from engaging in it with the Indians,"[37] which, of course, they did not.

Certainly the creation of the Kansas-Nebraska Territory in 1854 within the boundaries of the land reserved for Indians only two decades earlier encouraged judicial confusion and indecision. If, for example, a vendor of alcohol to Indians was a legal resident of Missouri (as most were), should he or she be tried in a Missouri state court or in a federal court in Kansas Territory, where the sale allegedly had taken place? "I simply want to be informed to whom the complaint is to be made," wrote Osage River Agent Alfred J. Vaughan to the Indian Office in St. Louis after an arrest he had made west of Missouri in 1855.[38] It was a reasonable request. But no official response was forthcoming, because by then it was plain to the Indian Office that Indian country as a place for protecting Indians from alcohol simply was not working, as evidenced by the suffering, the destitution, and especially the high mortality rates among the removal Indians. So said scores of government agents based on personal observation. And so also said private observers with no stake in the alcohol trade west of Missouri and Arkansas. One foreign traveler in 1855, for example, was absolutely dumbfounded at the traders' blatant disregard of and contempt for federal Indian law in Indian country:

> It seems almost impossible that a blind man, retaining the senses of smell, taste and hearing, could remain ignorant of a thing so palpably plain. The alcohol is put into wagons, at Westport or Independence [Missouri], *in open day-light,* and taken into the Territory, *in open day-light,* where it remains a week or more awaiting the arrival of its owners. Two government agents reside at Westport, while six or eight companies of Dragoons are stationed at Fort Leavenworth, ostensibly for the purpose of protecting the Indians and suppressing this infamous traffic,—and yet it suffers no diminution from *their vigilance!* What faithful public officers! How prompt in the discharge of their *whole* duty![39]

Similarly, tribal leaders on the Wyandot reservation, less than a day's travel from Independence and Fort Leavenworth, were described in 1856 as "drunken sots" and the tribal rank and file, as addicted to "drinking frolics," one of which led to the burning of the local Methodist missionary church, and all of which, according to U.S. Indian Agent William Gay, attributable to a white man who operated a "rum and whiskey store" on the very grounds of the Wyandot reservation.[40]

Inscribed in the federal statute books in the same year that the more stringent 1847 alcohol statute went into effect was another law that further compromised the increasingly unstable situation in Indian country. The movement of federal troops west during the early days of the Mexican-American War and the burgeoning white population of Oregon prompted the creation, on March 3, 1847, of two new mail routes directly across Indian country: one from Independence to Santa Fe, via Bent's Fort, and another from Independence to Astoria, near the mouth of the Columbia, by way of the Platte route.[41] These new routes constituted yet another federally directed invasion of Indian country, with stagecoaches carrying U.S. mail and passengers over these routes on a monthly basis by 1849, weekly by the mid-1850s, and daily by 1860. Rest and supply stations or so-called trading ranches operated by federally licensed traders sprang up all along the mail routes; for example, on the Santa Fe Trail there was the Diamond Spring Ranch, operated by Waldo, Hall & Co., with a contract to carry the mail from western Missouri to Santa Fe in 1849. There the Hall firm constructed a stone corral and several large stone buildings, including a hotel that served meals and was a place where "a thirsty traveler could drink something stronger than spring water." Similar facilities were established at Cottonwood Crossing, where freighters, overland travelers, and the military and Indians alike could obtain "brandy, Red Jacket Bitters, sweet wine, cognac, sherry claret, and barrels of whiskey," and at Cow Creek Crossing, where Asahel Beach and his son Abijah did "a considerable business in the grocery [i.e., alcohol] and provision line."[42]

Despite the 1847 law, the Indian alcohol business continued to flourish along the Oregon-California Trail, especially after the discovery of gold in California and the onset of the massive white migration to the mines in 1849. Writing from Iowa Point in present-day northeastern Kansas, Nemaha Subagent William P. Richardson reported in 1850 that the harvesting of corn and other crops among the Indians under his charge was far below normal as a result of the California emigrants providing "increased facilities to obtain ardent spirits." In the Texas border country to the south, the Chickasaws and other "civilized" tribes were able to obtain all the alcohol their cash or credit would allow at whiskey shops on the Texas side of Indian country or from vendors who plied the Red River by boat for the sole purpose of searching out new Indian clients. In fact so destructive had the annuity-driven alcohol business become by midcentury that one Indian agent advised that the "annuities of the many [tribes] afford certain data by which the final extinction of the red men could, with absolute arithmetical precision, be made. . . . I view annuities, in money paid to Indians, as a great misfortune, if not a curse." Indian Commissioner George W. Manypenny agreed. In his annual report of 1853 he singled out the Indian alcohol business as a monstrous

> violation of all law, human and divine; the fruitful source of crime and untold misery; and the frequent cause of serious brawls and disturbances upon the frontiers, as well as within the Indian country. It having been found that the Indians, on the faith of their annuities, frequently obtained liquor on credit . . . to the prejudice of the licensed and legitimate trades among the Indians, it is intended hereafter, as far as possible, to keep such persons out of the Indian country entirely, and especially at the time of the payments.[43]

But this tardy, indeed woeful, call for a new "fence" law contradicted reality dating back to the very inception of Indian country under the 1834 law, and in view of the creation of Kansas Territory less than one year later, was evidence that the *locus in quo* criterion, that is, the prohibition of alcohol sales to Indians in Indian country but not to Indians per se, was a categorical failure. Not surprisingly, then, the safe-place strategy for halting Indian drinking in Indian country came under congressional scrutiny and was finally abandoned, albeit temporarily, in January 1862, by an amendment to Section 20 of the trade and intercourse act of 1834, stipulating that the words "in the Indian country" following the word "Indian" in the law be deleted in favor of "under the charge of an Indian superintendent or Indian agent appointed by the United States."[44]

Twelve years later, however, Section 2139 of the *Revised Statutes* reinstated "Indian country" as the place where every person "except an Indian, in the Indian country" was prohibited from bringing alcohol into Indian country for sale or barter to any Indian under federal charge.[45] Was this Indian country the Indian country of 1834, especially in view of the several territories and states established within its exterior boundaries in the meantime? The answer is found in the first case to reach the Supreme Court regarding the location of Indian country as defined in 1834 (and amended thereafter), which was heard in 1877.[46] In this case the issue was whether the seizure of liquor by military authorities in Indian country as defined in Section 1 of the 1834 act was a legal action, the locus of the seizure being at a certain place in Dakota Territory. Writing for the court, Justice Samuel Freeman Miller held that although the incident unequivocally had taken place in Dakota Territory, that location, absent any legal abrogation of the original Indian title in the meantime, remained Indian country as described in the 1834 act. In what one authority on American Indian law has termed an "unusual opinion,"[47] Justice Miller concluded, as we have seen:[48]

Notwithstanding the immense changes which have taken place in the vast region covered by the act of 1834, by the extinguishment of Indian titles, the creation of States and the formation of territorial governments, Congress has not thought it necessary to make any new definition of Indian country. Yet during all this time a large body of laws has been in existence, whose operation was confined to the Indian country, *whatever that may be* [emphasis added]. And men have been punished by death, by fine, and by imprisonment, of which the courts who so punished them had no jurisdiction, if the offences were not committed in the Indian country as established by law. These facts afford the strongest presumption that the Congress of the United States, and the judges who administered those laws, must have found in the definition of Indian country, in the act of 1834, such an adaptability to the altered circumstances of what was then Indian country as to enable them to ascertain what it was at any time since then.[49]

Certainly the act's "adaptability to the altered circumstances" was evident in the lower Platte Valley as early as 1846, at the very time Congress was crafting the law passed in 1847 authorizing sentences of up to two years in prison for anyone convicted of introducing or even attempting to introduce alcohol into the Indian country. In this case, the issue was a patently illegal Mormon settlement on Omaha land near the mouth of the Platte and well within the boundaries of the Indian country, from the summer of 1846 to the spring of 1848. True, Indian Office officials protested against the settlement from the start, which at its zenith numbered nearly 10,000 persons and at one point had about 4,000 acres of land planted in corn. But it is also true that President James Polk yielded to Mormon lobbyist Thomas L. Kane by refusing to expel the Mormons in the spring of 1847 and allowing them to stay until they decided to resume their march west on their own terms a year later. Not only did the Mormons violate the Omahas' land rights and Indian country in general; they harvested Omaha timber at will and so depleted the game-animal resources that one federal official described the Omahas' land, which extended 100 miles north of the Platte and nearly the same distance west of the Missouri, as "more destitute of game than any other" in Indian country. And as an important footnote to such brazen but apparently acceptable disregard for federal law at the highest level in Washington, the Mormons took alcohol into Indian country as well. Indeed, such practice apparently was so prevalent that Brigham Young himself decreed that any of his followers who provided the Indians with alcohol would be whipped under official authority of the Mormon church.[50]

It would be simple and surely less cumbersome to dismiss the Mormon episode among the Omahas as an unfortunate but short-lived incident of no major or enduring significance for the under-standing of what was actually taking place in Indian country. But the Mormon invasion of the Omahas' land was a significant manifestation of what Judge Miller meant when invoking the instrument of "adaptability" as the proper way of understanding the true character of Indian country under the 1834 legislation. Successful in farming, hunting, and building in remote places, the well-publicized Mormon encampments in Indian country spoke powerfully to outsiders regarding the area's potential for non-Indian settlement. So wrote journalist Edwin Bryant while en route to California, as we have seen.[51] The soil there, on the Omaha lands and south into the Kansas and lower Republican river valleys, said Bryant, was "capable of producing every variety of crop adapted to this latitude." Others traveling west over the same terrain, including foreigners with no previous experience in America, concurred with Bryant's appraisal.[52] But in a gloomy and at times poetic commentary on the government's obvious failure to improve the lot of the Indians, Bryant also wrote: "They [the Indians] are now starving, and have turned pensioners upon the government of the United States, and beggars of the emigrants passing west. . . . Beautiful as the [Indian] country is, the silence and desolation reigning over it excites irrepressible emotions of sadness and melancholy."[53]

7

Compression

The failure of the Western Territory bill in 1834 was a severe blow to the security of the removal Indians in the trans-Missouri West, and when the House adjourned in 1838 without taking up the Senate's "Indian territorial bill,"[1] the issue was a dead letter even though there would be modest attempts to raise it in the future. Only the Indian Trade and Intercourse Act of 1834 remained what one authority on Jacksonian Indian policy has termed the "organic statute" for the area officially deemed Indian country by the federal government.[2] In fact the "strong fence" provided by the 1834 act was the Indians' best and only real defense for challenging the white migration to Oregon and California, the overland traffic to Santa Fe and Chihuahua, the movement of federal troops west during the Mexican-American War, and the proliferation of trails across the prairie-plains, where, ironically, Indians with native know-how often assisted novice or uninformed overland travelers, thereby providing comfort and added impetus for the non-Indian advance into Indian country.[3] Moreover, developments of this sort provided further justification for the revision of Indian policy, well under way in the mid-1840s,[4] regarding the compression of Indian land as a more effective means of promoting native economic, social, and moral improvement. As Indian country therefore became an ever more popular destination for outsiders, questions naturally arose regarding the permanence and flexibility of that place for its announced purpose under the 1834 law. For example, did a particular plot of ceded land in and of itself retain its legal status as Indian country after the ratification of an Indian cession treaty? Or did it revert to the public domain, absent any other legal Indian claim, as it must have existed prior to 1834? Essentially that had been the Supreme Court's ruling several decades later. Or did the plot evolve into some other cognizable legal status? As there was no serious discussion of such matters at the national level in the months and even years following passage of the 1834 act, it is necessary to rely on what little evidence is available, for example, a letter Secretary of War Cass sent to Indiana Indian Agent William Marshall less than two weeks after the Indian country law went into effect.

After a preliminary declaration indicating that the Indiana delegation in Congress had demanded that "another effort should be made to procure a cession of the Miami and Potawatomi reservations in that State," and that this was agreeable to President Jackson as long as the new arrangement would cost the government no more money, Cass called Agent Marshall's attention to a map enclosed for such purposes, entitled "Map of the western Region approximated for the Emigrating Indians." There the Osage and Kansa cessions of 1825 were clearly designated "vacant," thus providing a pliant designation for the land in question and, by extension, Indian country in general. And for the removal of the Miamis and Potawatomis to Indian country with dispatch, which was the government's ultimate objective, Cass informed Agent Marshall that

the country between the Osage reservations and the Arkansas Territory with a small exception is *vacant* as is the country between the Osages & Shawnees. The land between the Platte and Kickapoo reservation is also *vacant* as well as an extensive tract North West of that assigned to the Illinois Potawatomies. The Wyandots of Ohio, the New York Indians & and the Potawatomies of Indiana are the only Eastern Tribes whose Western location is not specifically provided for, and the Miamis and the Potawatomies may be placed upon either of the said tracts unless the same should be previously selected by the Wyandots. . . . It is supposed that the payment of annuities will afford you a favorable opportunity for bringing the matter to a close[5] (emphasis added).

And certainly it did. Together, the Miamis and Potawatomis were given $210,800 for their Indiana land plus new homes about 600 miles west, on land that in the interim had apparently been returned to its original Indian country status.[6] For the government the ceding of Indian land by treaty was, of course, an attractive and flexible tool for accommodating white land hunger in the East while filling in "vacant" country in the West with the emigrant tribes from the East. But as we shall see, designating ceded Indian country land simply as "vacant" land, no matter the time or extent of that designation, would only complicate the questions of what and where Indian country was at any given time. Indeed, such action would come back to haunt the partisans of tribal land compression.

It is important to understand that the government's avowed concern for tribal economic development and moral improvement was not the only engine of change in Indian country. Nearly a century ago James C. Malin called attention to an 1846 government report of St. Louis Indian Superintendent Thomas H. Harvey stating that, in reference to the Peoria lands near the Missouri border and south of the Kansas River, it would be benevolent policy "to extinguish the Indian title to the lands that they have no need of, whenever it [could] be done on advantageous terms and with benefit to the Indians." Continued Malin, quoting Commissioner of Indian Affairs William Medill's annual report of 1848, the regrettable consequence of the white advance into Indian country was collusion with Indians and thus an impediment for improving them and rescuing them from a savage state to a civilized one, surely a major objective of the government's removal program. The solution, however, was not to interdict the white invasion but to consolidate the intervening Indians into compact groups. Under this new arrangement the administration of Indian policy would be more efficient and effective, and if this "great end" were accomplished, insisted Commissioner Medill,

> material changes will soon have to be made in the position of some of the smaller tribes on the frontier [i.e., Indian country], so as to leave an ample outlet for our white population. . . . It may be said that we have commenced the establishment of two colonies for the Indians that have been compelled to remove; one north, on the headwaters of the Mississippi, and the other south, on the western borders of Missouri and Arkansas, the southern limit of which is the Red river.

It was a clarion call for a dramatic shift in Indian policy, emphasized Malin. The new policy, which had been contemplated for some time, would allow the clearing of the Platte and Kansas valleys of Indians. Then a passage could be opened for the central railroad route to the Pacific, and "a great fertile country for the extension of the frontier" would become available.7

More recently Robert A. Trennert, Jr., moved well beyond Malin's work and analyzed Indian affairs in Texas, New Mexico, the high plains Indian occupancy areas designated by the Fort Laramie treaty of 1851, and, to lesser degree, the reservation country of the border tribes. Trennert concluded that the idea of moving Indians away from land attractive to white settlement "had been brewing for some time," and significant steps toward the formulation of a more general reservation system for Indians were taken in the years 1846–1851.[8] Building on Trennert's conclusion that compression had been "brewing for some time," there is good evidence that a significant step toward the reservation system had been taken as early as 1825, when treaties with the Kansas and Osages had created sixty-three reservations of 640 acres each for the half-bloods of those tribes, twenty-three for the Kansas and forty for the Osages (and in the case of the Kansas alone, the treaty reduced their total tribal holdings by more than 16,000,000 acres[9]), with millions more to be relinquished in 1846. That these were in fact reasonable Indian land compressions and thus part of the government's design for Indian improvement in Indian country (and possibly the eventual opening of a central railroad route as well) were justified in the words of William Clark, who wrote in 1825:

Each of the treaties contain several reservations of a mile square in favor of [the Osage and Kansa] half-breed Indians and their children. Reserves of this kind have heretofore been made in behalf of such persons and in my opinion have a good effect in promoting civilization as their attachment is created to a fixed residence and an idea of separate property is imparted without which it is vain to think of improving the minds and morals of the Indians or making progress in the work of civilization. . . . Experience having convinced me of the necessity of preventing a white and Indian population from remaining in immediate contact with each other and the Indians themselves fully sensible of the inconveniences of such neighborhoods, it has been stipulated . . . that the Osage reservation shall commence twenty miles west of the Missouri line and the Kanzas about double that distance.[10]

The government had therefore entered into tribal land compression well in advance of moving eastern Indians into the new Indian country, thus providing ample time for evaluating just how well such compression might contribute to their improvement. For that purpose the selection of the diminished reservations, beginning on the fertile and well-timbered banks of the Kansas River near present-day downtown Topeka and extending 23 miles east, could not have been more attractively situated for the transition to subsistence agriculture and, perhaps, commercial farming and urban development as well.

But Clark, as it turned out, was wrong. Writing to the Indian Office in 1840, St. Louis Indian Superintendent Joshua Pilcher reported that most of the Kansa grantees resided in St. Louis, where they repeatedly besieged his office for permission to sell their reserves to white speculators. Two years later, Pilcher's successor advised that the half-breed Kansas "were so destitute that selling their land was their only alternative,"[11] even though such action was prohibited by law.[12] By 1848, squatters and timber merchants from nearby Missouri were invading their lands with impunity.[13]

In the meantime, by the Osage treaty of 1839, the Osage half-breed grantees were allowed to sell their 640-acre reservations to the government for a sum "not exceeding two dollars per acre,"[14] with the result that the tribe as a whole was able to fend off the compression of their remaining Indian country land until the mid-1860s. The Kansas, however, were less fortunate. In 1846 they were persuaded to cede an additional 6,559,040 acres in exchange for a new annuity fund and a 20-mile-square reservation near Council Grove on the upper Neosho,[15] not because they were making progress toward the white man's "civilization" as Superintendent Clark had forecast two decades earlier, but simply because they were destitute and owners of some of the finest land in all of Indian country. After a hasty and as it turned out incorrect survey of the new reservation,

Superintendent Harvey advised authorities in Washington that the "degenerate and docile" Kansas would take up residence at Council Grove within a matter of days. In fact the tribe spent the fall and early winter of 1847–1848 begging and stealing from the emigrant tribes, as well as from military personnel at Fort Leavenworth and wholly unsympathetic whites along the western border of Missouri. Not until late January 1848 were emergency provisions provided and the Kansas finally directed to their new and much-compressed reservation on the upper Neosho.[16]

By then the government's program for removing Indians to Indian country had been completed. Selected bands (or in some cases total populations) of the Sacs and Foxes, Kickapoos, Delawares, Shawnees, Wyandots, Potawatomis, Ottawas, Miamis, Peorias, Kaskaskias, Weas, Piankashaws, and New York Indians had been placed in the area east of the ninety-eighth meridian between the thirty-seventh and fortieth parallels, whereas most of the terrain south of the thirty-seventh parallel and east of the hundredth meridian was assigned by "perpetual" treaty guarantees to the Cherokee, Choctaw, Creek, Seminole, and Chickasaw people. And in the meantime, by an 1833 treaty, the Pawnees ceded title to their lands south of the Platte, thus adding significantly to the amount of unassigned Indian country land cleared of legal Indian title by the Kansa cessions of 1825 and 1846. By 1848, then, excluding the thirteen removal reservations established in a checkerboard manner immediately west of Missouri, there were millions of acres of "vacant" or what James C. Malin described as "land free from Indian title" in Indian country,[17] in present-day eastern Kansas and north into Nebraska south of the Platte.

For what purpose? To accommodate more emigrant Indians? To provide more land for the removal Indians already there? For the benefit of certain plains tribes to the west and north that under the Fort Laramie treaty of 1851 were awarded specific occupancy areas?

For a reasonable response to these and similar questions, it is important to consider the yearnings, indeed demands, of non-Indians, and it is therefore important to return to the Kansa treaty of 1846. Article 5 of the treaty provided that if the president of the United States determined that an insufficient supply of timber was available within the proposed relocation area (as designated in Article 5), he was empowered "to cause to be selected a suitable country, near the western boundary of the land ceded by this treaty, which shall remain for their use forever."[18] Three months after the treaty was proclaimed, Superintendent Harvey announced that, in addition to a lack of timber on the unceded location near the junction of the Republican and Smoky Hill rivers, the settlement site was too close to the hostile Pawnees, and that the Kansas on their part were no less concerned after learning that an unfriendly Comanche war party had only recently traveled through the area. Harvey therefore decided that the upper Neosho Valley, around 30 miles to the southeast of the Republican–Smoky Hill junction, was a better location, and at least some of the Kansa leadership and a few warriors had agreed to this. Since Harvey favored the area in and around Council Grove, a major Santa Fe Trail outfitting station and retail center with much potential for further development, he directed Fort Leavenworth Agent Richard W. Cummins to locate the actual reservation boundaries with an eye for *future disposition of the unappropriated land adjacent to the reservation* (emphasis added).[19]

Precisely who was to benefit from the "unappropriated land" was not spelled out by Harvey, but that it was attractive for white settlement was corroborated by a prominent government explorer with extensive travel experience in the trans-Missouri and Rocky Mountain West. Recounting his recent march from western Missouri to the upper Arkansas via the Kansas and Smoky Hill valleys for the purpose of locating a pass that would accommodate the central (or thirty-eighth parallel) transcontinental railroad route over the Continental Divide, ex-Lieutenant John C. Fremont wrote from Bent's Fort on November 16, 1848: "We find that the valley of the Kanzas affords by far the most eligible approach to the mountains. The whole valley soil is of a very superior quality, and the route very direct. . . . This line would afford *continuous and good settlements* [emphasis added] certainly for four hundred miles, and is therefore worthy of consideration in any plan of approach to the mountains."[20]

Thus it is clear that Harvey's vision for "unappropriated land" near Council Grove and Fremont's call for "continuous and good settlements" hundred of miles farther west were as much for non-Indians as for Indians, even though the terrain in question remained Indian country in 1848 as much as it was in 1834. And as if to complement such express encouragement for white settlements in Indian country, the government authorized, on May 11, 1850, regular mail service between Independence and Santa Fe. The first four-year, $72,000 contract—supplemented by a government license to engage in the Indian trade—went to Waldo, Hall & Co. of Independence, Missouri, a veteran government contractor, which established a farm, depot, and "traveling post" at Council Grove. Waldo, Hall & Co. also "sent out a blacksmith, a number of men to cut and cure hay, with a quantity of animals, grain and provisions," thus confirming Superintendent Harvey's report that the land in and around Council Grove was indeed available for non-Indian use and settlement.[21]

But was not the area still Indian country and thus off limits to all non-Indians except those specifically designated in the Indian Trade and Intercourse Act of 1834 or authorized by treaties such as the ones concluded with the Osages and Kansas in 1825? Was not the government's removal program designed to protect the removal Indians from outside interference while Indian agents, teachers, agriculturists, missionary organizations, and other so-called humanitarian societies—all under the watchful eye of their benevolent Great Father in Washington—delivered civilization to the uncivilized? Potawatomi

Agent George W. Clarke thought so and in 1854 demanded that the government take action against employees of Waldo, Hall & Co. for "taking claims" to Indian land near Council Grove and the diminished Kansa reservation.[22] Whether officials in Washington (or in St. Louis) responded to Clarke is not known; if they did, their response (or a copy of their response) was not placed or retained in the files of the Indian Office. Less debatable is that the myth of a "vacant" Indian country, the appeal of "unappropriated land" adjacent to Indian land, and the compression of tribal land on the model of what happened at Council Grove in 1848 provided the impetus and means for a more aggressive and widespread intrusion of Indian country in the decade to come.[23]

8

Intrusion

In a widely quoted letter dated December 17, 1853, that was sent to supporters of a convention to be held in St. Joseph, Missouri, for the purpose of promoting a new territory in Indian country to be called "Nebraska," Senator Stephen A. Douglas asserted that "the Indian barrier must be removed." Confronted with "a wilderness fifteen hundred miles in breadth, filled with hostile savages," America had to protect its possessions and interests on the Pacific by eliminating this troublesome barrier. Taking his conclusion as indisputable fact, the Illinois senator continued:

> Lines of settlement with civil, political and religious institutions all under the protection of law, are imperiously demanded by the national considerations. These are essential, but they are not sufficient. No man can keep up with the spirit of this age who travels on anything slower than the locomotive, and fails to receive intelligence by lightning. . . . The removal of the Indian barrier and the extension of the law of the United States in the form of Territorial governments are the first steps toward the accomplishment of each and all of these objects.[1]

Thus what Potawatomi Chief Quish-Queh-Leh had been assured two decades earlier was a strong fence behind which "all the Indians towards the setting sun, from the State of Missouri, would be secured in their possessions,"[2] was now seen as a troublesome barrier to the security and progress of the United States.

Not all agreed with this position, certainly not during the debate leading to passage of the Kansas-Nebraska Act of May 30, 1854. Senator William H. Seward, of New York, for example, suggested it was unwise to establish territorial government in Nebraska because of the eighteen tribes living there, fourteen of which were there as a consequence of the government's actions alone. "Where will they go?" he asked. "Back across the Mississippi? . . . To the Himalayas?"[3] Regarding the emigrant Indians already resident in Indian country, Congressman Samuel H. Walley, of Massachusetts, likewise emphasized that they were there not by choice but by the government's own demands and actions:

> Yes sir, wave after wave has rolled in upon the helpless Indian; he has been driven back; he has made a stand; he has asserted his rights; bargained for a new position; receded back to occupy it; been overtaken by the ever-pressing tide rolling westward and farther west. . . . But, Mr. Chairman, again the sea is lashed into a storm; again the ocean roar is heard. . . . Methinks I see the Indian urged on by the advancing wave, pressing still westward, till he finds himself in view of the vast ocean, and, as his eyes look in vain for other lands to which he may retire, he feels the force of the waves of the Pacific turned against him, and pressing him backward toward the Rocky Mountains.[4]

In contrast, white farmers and speculators, as well as the transcontinental railroad interests who urged them onward, viewed Indian

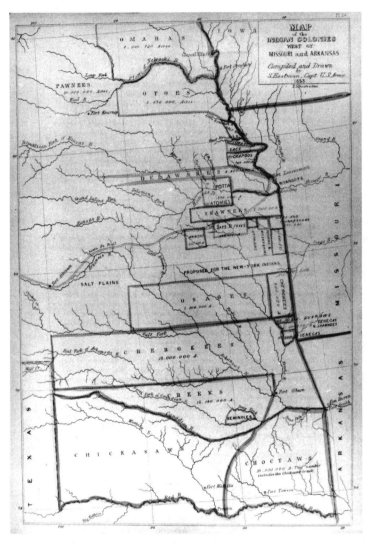

"Map of the Indian Colonies West of Missouri and Arkansas, Compiled and Drawn by S. Eastman, Capt. U.S. Army, 1853," similar to the map Indian Commissioner George W. Manypenny provided Senator Thomas Hart Benton for distribution to potential non-Indian settlers in Indian country. Courtesy Department of Special Collections, Ablah Library, Wichita State University.

country as a land of opportunity, not as a place for tribal security and moral improvement. Based on his travels through Indian country in 1854, Edward Everett Hale observed that poverty and misery were the "normal condition" there. In fact the Indians were "their own worst enemies," said Hale, and their number was "diminishing so rapidly that even had they ever needed all this land they could not now occupy it."[5]

Similar to Hale's assessment was that of the Reverend C. B. Boynton and T. B. Mason, based on personal observations in Indian country that same year. Noting that the Delaware lands near Fort Leavenworth were valued at $50 to $60 an acre and that squatters were occupying these lands with impunity, Boynton and Mason announced that although the Indian country reservations constituted "an inconsiderable portion of the Territory in quantity," they actually incorporated some of the most fertile and best-timbered terrain west of the Missouri. However, the Indians' neglect of this valuable resource was sure evidence of their inability to travel the right road toward economic security and human fulfillment, and therefore it was "wholly impossible that these lands should be long held by the Indian tribes as they now are."[6] And as if to underscore native deficiency at its worst, they focused on the Kaw (Kansa) tribe, onetime owners of millions of acres in Indian country and once regarded with enough respect to cause the U.S. government to request their permission for locating and marking a highway across their domain to Mexico, but now confined to a 20-mile-square reservation near Council Grove. Wrote Boynton and Mason, not only to satisfy their obvious racist proclivities but in broader perspective for the benefit of an increasing number of easterners interested in western land and the unsettled situation in Indian country as well:

They [the Kaw Indians] are among the lowest and poorest of the Indian tribes—guilty of all the vices that Paul ascribes to heathenism, in the first chapter of Romans—and if any new wickedness has been invented since Paul wrote, they doubtless have learned even that. . . . The difference between an encampment of these heathen Kaws, and a Christian community, no mathematics can calculate. The scene [at Council Grove] was enough to stagger one's belief in the unity of the race. . . . Their probation as a community is over, their judgment day even is passed; *nationally*, they are among the lost.[7]

Of particular significance was the assertion that the Kaws' downfall had taken place "*nationally*," that their future as a *national* entity was a thing of the past, and that a similar fate awaited other Indian people in Indian country as well. Commenting on the government's having dispatched a senior official to Indian country to advance such a point of view in 1853, a prominent eastern newspaper wrote that a majority of the Indian country tribes would "probably surrender their lands on terms such as the Government can accept without disadvantage," and that barring possibly "mischievous" actions on the part of "selfish white men," no difficulties were anticipated in the "transfer of Indian [land] rights to the Government."[8]

The official sent to Indian country in the late summer of 1853 was Indian Commissioner George W. Manypenny, armed with the authority of a law passed by Congress the previous March 3 providing a $50,000 appropriation for new land cession and/or allotment treaties to clear the way for a transcontinental railroad, stimulate the organization of a Kansas-Nebraska Territory, and, perhaps, promote the non-Indian settlement of Indian country as well.[9] Manypenny seemed a wise choice for the assignment. He was a prominent Ohio publisher, lawyer, businessman, and respected politician who had lost the Democrat nomination for his state's governorship by only three votes in 1853, and who was viewed on both sides of the aisle as a trusted community leader and good party man, well informed regarding the major social and economic issues of the time. Once in office, however, Manypenny surprised land-hungry western farmers and the railroad crowd alike by announcing that none of the land west of the Missouri and Iowa was legally open to non-Indian settlement.[10]

Despite one eastern newspaper's contention that after some initial "excitement," most potential settlers with an eye on Indian country land displayed a readiness "to await patiently the action of the Government,"[11] Commissioner Manypenny's report to Interior Secretary Robert McClelland painted a much less rosy picture. For one thing, said Manypenny, the principal spokesmen of the sixteen tribal councils, representing more than 14,000 Indians, the Indians displayed no inclination "to play diplomat on the subject of their lands" but rather armed themselves, organized a grand council, and threatened to form a confederation to "light up their fires after the old Indian fashion."

Continued Manypenny in his report to the Interior Department, "They [the tribal leaders] were shown [maps] of California and Oregon and the settlements, and were shown how they were in the way of the [railroad] routes in their present location." They were also told that the buffalo supply would soon be "cut off," leaving the Indians no alternative but to "work as white men." But the Indians reminded the commissioner of past promises that their "present location would be their permanent home." In fact, said Manypenny, "the main speaker in every council put this point forward." "I admitted to this," he acknowledged, "but said that their true interests demanded that this be changed."[12]

According to Manypenny's report, the Indians had failed to take advantage of the government's myriad benevolence, and too many Indians were intemperate, indolent, and generally degraded. They also had failed to take advantage of what the missionaries and other white men of goodwill had to offer, and in any case the flood of white settlers to Oregon and California and the consequent decline of the buffalo herd meant that the time had come for them to take advantage of what the government had to offer and to pattern their lives on the model of the white man. "I could have made treaties with several tribes," Manypenny claimed, "but only on condition that each should receive for a tribal home that part of their land adjoining the states," a condition that he rejected outright on grounds that such an arrangement was in the best interests of neither the Indians nor the whites. Above all else, Manypenny's trip to Indian country had convinced him that "a civil government should be erected over any new Indian territory" and that the Indian Trade and Intercourse Act of 1834, originally designed to create a more manageable and permanent Indian country, was, in fact, a *"dead letter"* (emphasis added).[13]

Strong and far-reaching words, certainly from the ranking member of the Office of Indian Affairs. But there were reasons beyond Manypenny's mission to Indian country that prompted him to view Indian country as a relic of the past. Certainly in mid-1853 it required no divine direction to understand that territorial government, with or without slavery, would soon be in place west of Missouri and Iowa. Whether it would encompass the entire Indian country as defined in 1834 or only as far west as the ninety-eighth meridian, which Isaac McCoy had designated "favorable for settlement" in 1830,[14] was uncertain. But a veritable army of land-hungry white farmers, land speculators, and corporate boosters poised on the eastern border of Indian country and believing in the wise use of nature's bounty was simply unwilling to accept the idea that millions of acres of fertile farm land would remain off limits, or that a handful of so-called barrier Indian reservations could hamper or even block the transcontinental railroad.

At stake, then, were valuable material resources demanding development. And from a different but not less significant perspective, in

1851 the almost poetic pronouncements of Indiana Representative George W. Julian on the House floor, regarding the virtues of agrarian life, were comforting words to politicians in Washington and would-be pioneer yeomen anxiously awaiting the opportunity to possess the fertile river bottoms, the majestic groves of hardwoods, and the prolific prairies of Indian country:

> The life of the farmer is peculiarly favorable to virtue, and both individuals and communities are generally happy in proportion as they are virtuous. His manners are simple, and his nature unsophisticated. If not oppressed by other interests, he generally possesses an abundance without the drawback of luxury. His life does not impose excessive toil, and yet it discourages idleness. The farmer lives in rustic plenty, remote from the contagion of popular vices, and enjoys, in their greatest fruition, the blessings of health and contentment. . . . The pleasures and virtues of rural life have been the theme of poets and philosophers in all ages. The tillage of the soil was the primeval employment of man. Of all arts, it is the most useful and necessary. It has justly been styled the nursing father of the State; for in civilized countries all are equally dependent upon it for the means of subsistence.[15]

With such powerful forces at work it was hardly surprising that soon after Commissioner Manypenny took office in the spring of 1853 his feet would be held to the fire regarding the permanence and inviolability of Indian country. Igniting and then stoking the blaze was veteran Congressman Thomas Hart Benton of Missouri, lawyer, outspoken frontier editor, retired army officer, celebrated "prophet of American expansion,"[16] and champion of a central transcontinental railroad route that, with anticipated federal assistance, would benefit his own state of Missouri. Benton, who had been one of Missouri's first senators (1821–1851) and chairman of the Senate Committee on Indian Affairs during the Monroe administration,[17] was widely viewed as one of the most informed and influential public figures on Indian policy and Indian affairs at that time.

As chairman of the powerful Indian committee, Senator Benton had worked closely with Superintendent Clark in St. Louis and Secretary Cass in Washington during the prolonged and often contentious proceedings leading to passage of the Indian Removal Act of 1830 and the 1834 law creating Indian country. Indeed, Benton had been at the very epicenter of the issues and the political maneuvering these laws and related treaties involved, including the enormous land cessions Superintendent Clark had secured from the Osages and Kansas in 1825, thereby prompting expectations in the Indian Office that Congressman Benton's knowledge of the objectives, the essential characteristics, and especially the legal boundaries of Indian country would conform to, or at least reflect in some manner, the knowledge he had gained while heading the Senate Indian Committee three decades earlier. In the fall of 1853, however, Commissioner Manypenny learned otherwise, thus setting the stage for a confrontation with Benton and sundry expansionists determined to destroy the "strong fence" established by law in 1834.

Years later Commissioner Manypenny recalled that Representative Benton "had made a publication [in 1853], taking the ground that a large portion of the [Indian] country was then subject to the occupancy of the whites, without the consent of the Indians or the aid of congressional legislation," allegedly based on a map of the Nebraska country prepared under the supervision of Commissioner Manypenny in response to a request from Benton to the Indian Office in 1853. According to Manypenny, however, the map was an outright fraud first shown to him by certain unidentified "exploring parties" during his trip to Indian country that same year. "He had never prepared a map for any such purpose" and in fact there was "not one acre of land" then open to settlement in the entire Indian country, insisted Manypenny.[18]

Commissioner Manypenny had been in Indian country from September 2 until October 11, 1853,[19] and therefore, he was not privy to the day-to-day correspondence coming into the Indian Office, which apparently included Congressman Benton's request for the Indian country map. But that there was mounting pressure for opening Indian country to white settlement surely came as no surprise to Manypenny. Less than a month prior to his departure for Indian country he had received a letter from Missouri Senator David R. Atchison, arch political rival of Benton and member of the Committee on Indian Affairs, asking whether any land lying west of Iowa and Missouri, that is, in the proposed Nebraska Territory—and, of course, in the Indian country—could be "occupied" by white settlers. Though noting that the Osage and Kansa nations had relinquished title to a large body of land west of Iowa and Missouri as early as 1825, Manypenny was adamant in his response that "no portion of the proposed Territory of Nebraska [was] open for settlement legally." "We are trying to extinguish [Indian land titles]," explained Manypenny to Senator Atchison, "and we hope no one will take action which will embarrass the government in this."[20]

But to challenge Manypenny at all costs was Benton's strategy. By convincing the Indian commissioner to agree that *all* Indian country land not specifically granted to the emigrant tribes, to the Osages, Kansas, and Pawnees as compensation for their pre-1834 cessions, or to other Indian nations since 1834, for example, portions of the upper Platte, Republican, and Arkansas valleys excluded by the Cheyenne and Arapaho lands granted by the Fort Laramie Treaty of 1851,[21] the commissioner would have to agree that such country was in fact open to white settlement, as long as such settlement did not violate the public domain laws of the United States. And to strengthen his cause, Benton obtained the support of other Missouri or frontier notables, including Democratic Congressman William P. Hall, member of the House Committee on Public Lands, the support of which was necessary for any significant change in the public domain code; Abelard Guthrie, an aggressive member of the Wyandot tribe (by marriage) and powerful Washington lobbyist who viewed himself as the best qualified candidate for delegate to Congress should the Nebraska Territory become a reality; and Lucian J. Eastin, editor-owner of the St. Joseph (Missouri) *Gazette* and the Leavenworth (Kansas Territory) *Kansas Weekly Herald,* who helped organize a squatters' association and then presided over one of its meetings in Indian country across the Missouri River from St. Joseph in 1854.[22]

With the assistance of Guthrie, Eastin prepared a map of Indian country marking its exterior boundaries or, as Benton put it, only "an outline of the whole." The map was then sent to Commissioner Manypenny's office in Washington with a cover letter requesting that the boundaries of the Osage and Kansa cessions of 1825, the Pawnee cession of 1833, and the emigrant reserves dating back to the beginning of the government's removal program be drawn in and clearly labeled. In Manypenny's absence his clerks in the Indian Office complied as best they could and returned the revised map to Benton, who had copies lithographed by the Jul. Hutawa firm in St. Louis, but with the added caption, "Official Map of the Indian Reservations in Nebraska Territory, drawn by the Commissioner of Indian Affairs at the request of Col. Benton, and published to show the *public lands* [emphasis added] subject to settlement." Although hundreds of copies of the map were distributed to potential Indian country settlers, mainly by newspapers such as Eastin's St. Joseph *Gazette,* Benton took to the speaker's platform in Missouri with the "astonishing" announcement that "new intelligence" from Washington indicated that the "whole country from the Missouri [river] to the Rocky Mountains, with the exception of a few Indian reservations—covering only about one fourth of the ground—is now open to settlement!" In fact the land was "free from Indian title," asserted Benton, "and from its beauty, fertility, salubrity and geographical position must speedily attract the preemptor and cultivator." Thus caught off guard, Manypenny retaliated with a strong letter to the Missouri press denouncing the Benton map as "well calculated to deceive the reader." In fact, said Manypenny, all the Indian country west of Missouri was closed to non-Indian settlement and the Benton map should be either ignored or withdrawn from circulation.[23]

From Senator Atchison, who Congressman Benton and his crowd believed was in league with Manypenny for the purpose of preventing the area west of Missouri from becoming a free-soil territory, came support for the beleaguered Indian commissioner. Responding to Benton's insistence that Senator Atchison opposed additional cession treaties for no other reason than to see Indian country "sunk in hell, before it shall become a free-soil territory," Atchison fired back by charging that the Osage, Kansa, and Pawnee cessions existed for no other reason than for "locating other Indians, [and] that it was by both parties so understood, and not for the purpose of settling white men."[24] An impasse between the Bentonites and the Manypenny forces was thus reached by the time the Kansas-Nebraska bill was signed into law, on May 30, 1854, and the program to promote railroads, farms, towns, preemption, or anything else that might expedite the white advance into Indian country at the expense of the Indians was alive and well.

Who was right? Looking backward from the Supreme Court's 1877 ruling, that Indian country remained Indian country as long as the Indians in question retained "original title" to their land and ceased to be Indian country whenever that "title" was lost, "in the absence of any different provision by treaty or by act of Congress," it would appear that the Osage, Kansa, and Pawnee cessions were fair game for white squatters, absent any part of these cessions having been designated for other purposes by treaty or congressional enactment. Moreover, the federal law of July 22, 1854,[25] extending preemption to *unsurveyed* lands of the public domain, as long as the Indian title had been relinquished, served as an added inducement to the squatters, as did the claim that ceded Indian land ipso facto was in the public domain. There was, of course, the old law of March 3, 1807, authorizing the use of force for the expulsion of intruders on ceded Indian lands, but the value of this law was minimized by the acting secretary of the interior, who in 1854 advised President Franklin Pierce:

> The bold and enterprising have for a long period of years been not only permitted, but encouraged by the general policy of the government with regard to the public lands to press forward in advance of the more natural and steady progress of settlement, and secure as a reward for the hardship and expenses they incurred, more valuable land for themselves. Indeed, so frequently has Congress enacted laws for the protection of persons who have settled on the public lands, prior to such settlements authorized by law, that the Act of 1807 has long since been lost sight of or regarded as obsolete.[26]

In short, a combination of the 1825 and 1833 land cessions, the extension of preemption to the ceded land absent formal government survey, and the claimed obsolescence of the 1807 intruder law provided the squatters with a powerful arsenal for invading the promised land, strong fence or not. To them it did not matter that the *ceded* Osage, Kansa, and Pawnee lands, an immense domain of more than 30 million acres in the Arkansas, Smoky Hill, Solomon, Neosho, and Republican watersheds of present-day Kansas and north of the Platte in present-day Nebraska, in the very heart of the area that Benton insisted was open to settlement, remained part of Indian country under Section 20 of the Indian Trade and Intercourse Act of

1834 and therefore off limits to the squatters. Thus with credit to Benton (and his retinue) for having bested Indian Commissioner Manypenny with their contrivance and selective untruths, the white invasion of Indian country proceeded as contemplated, prompting Delaware Agent Benjamin F. Robinson to inquire of his superiors in the Central Superintendency in St. Louis, "Are treaties merely made for fun, and hence to be looked on as maneuvers played off, for the benefit of a hungry crowd of land speculators?"[27]

An example of how the invasion was actually carried out may be seen on the Kickapoo reservation, in what is now Doniphan County, Kansas, directly across the Missouri River from St. Joseph. On April 21, 1854, a Kickapoo delegation in company with their agent, Daniel Vanderslice, left for Washington to negotiate a land cession treaty, which was agreed to and signed by the Kickapoos and Commissioner Manypenny on May 18. Back in Indian country, from a site on the reservation near the present town of Wathena, trader Benjamin Harding wrote, "As soon as [Agent] Vanderslice left, many [persons] flocked over [the Missouri River] and made their claims by laying a foundation for a cabin and writing their names on a tree near by, and now [May 27] there is not even a grease spot left unclaimed [on the reservation] within my knowledge; and still claim hunters are passing daily. After thus locating their claims most of them go back and are now awaiting the results of the treaty."[28]

A year later, the efforts of Kansa Agent John Montgomery to expel intruders on the Kansa half-blood lands near present-day Topeka met with such resistance that he finally resorted to the burning of more than a dozen cabins on the half-blood lands, only to be threatened with arrest by the Douglas County sheriff on a charge of arson. Failing to receive the support of District Attorney General Andrew J. Isaacs or from military authorities at nearby Fort Leavenworth, Montgomery retreated to his agency headquarters at Council Grove, where he penned a letter to Indian Office authorities in St.

Louis, stating, "Where a certain class of people assume themselves the right to judge matters pertaining to Indian country, it is very difficult for an Indian agent to perform with promptness the duties of his office."[29]

A no less important variation of the white invasion was presented in a report of Indian Agent George Clarke to the Interior Department in 1856 regarding the manner in which the Potawatomi Indians viewed the performance of a Southern Baptist missionary working his craft in their midst. "The Indians charge often that Rev. John Jackson is influenced by no motive to advance the conditions of the Potawatomies or to promote education but that the motive most apparent from his operations is that of money making, speculation and a desire to get a foothold on the property of the Mission in case of a treaty."[30] It is clear that the intrusion of Indian country by non-Indians had become commonplace by the summer of 1854 and that the advent of civil institutions under authority of the Kansas-Nebraska Act offered little or no relief from such illegality.[31] Indeed, the result was quite the opposite. Less than a month after the 1854 act became law an obviously elated promoter of the Whitehead town site, planned for development in what is now northeastern Kansas, reported that "thousands have already come in, and thousands are still coming. The lands, for some ten to twenty miles back, have, with few exceptions been claimed by the squatters."[32] Another potential settler reported: "We have made one short trip over into Indian country, and satisfied ourselves that a man can get almost just the home as he pleases. I never saw richer land in my life; and it appears absolutely inexhaustible."[33] In fact, wrote "Philos" from St. Joseph in the summer of 1854, "Emigration to these [Kansas and Nebraska] territories is unprecedented except in the history of California."[34]

In sum, it was the land intended for the benefit of no one except Indians that was the main attraction. And it was this supposedly "inexhaustible" resource that caught the eye of Andrew H. Reeder, who was appointed governor of Kansas Territory on June 29, 1854, and who was removed from office a year later for speculating in the very lands that had been granted to the mixed-bloods of the Kansa nation for their own use in 1825, and also—as Superintendent William Clark had then emphasized—as a model for the improvement of the tribe as a whole.[35]

9

Illusion

Between 1854 and 1860, more than 100,000 non-Indians entered Kansas Territory to establish farms and town sites,[1] and to secure railroad rights-of-way west to the Continental Divide and beyond, lending credence to the belief that the creation of the territory constituted a blow of such severity that Indian country between the thirty-seventh and fortieth parallels was simply unable to survive. "Good as the intentions of the federal officials were in attempting to provide permanent homes for the Indians," suggested a widely cited general history of Indian-white relations in the United States, the government nevertheless was "powerless—or lacked the will to exert power—to fulfill promises to protect the Indians" when it was confronted with aggressive land speculators and the violence accompanying Bleeding Kansas. But of course it was the government that had made Kansas Territory out of Indian country in the first place, and it was the government that had extended preemption rights to Indian country land before it was officially surveyed, thus encouraging the speculators. And it was the government that had granted fee-simple allotments to selected Indians on grounds that such generosity would promote cultural improvement among the less fortunate members of their respective tribes. And no less important, it was the government that had designed and then executed the strategy for the emigrant Indians' relocation to Indian country. That the government was powerless or simply incapable of responding to the Indians' needs in a sensitive and constructive manner is at best disgraceful and difficult to understand, and that the government's power could be so diminished as to allow what happened in Indian country over the next decades is equally shameful.

What happened west of Missouri after 1854 was a revival of the government's removal program in a manner not widely publicized or understood in terms of its more avaricious and exploitative details. This time the removal was to the less attractive and therefore less marketable land south of the thirty-seventh parallel assigned to the Cherokees two decades earlier. The result was that, excluding a few "enduring" Indians who were able to accommodate the white invaders while retaining certain core components of their traditional culture, Indian country west of Missouri and Iowa as a safe place for Indians was reduced to a state of near emptiness by the mid-1870s.[2]

The driving forces behind such change came from two separate but related quarters. One, already alluded to, was best described by John C. McCoy, federal contractor (like his father, the Baptist missionary and removal partisan Isaac McCoy) for surveying reservations in Indian country. "The Territory of Kansas," McCoy wrote to the Indian Office in the fall of 1855, "is now filled with shrewd, designing and unscrupulous men who have a thousand different schemes concocted and in consequence there seems to be a perfect mania for acquiring lands—not only among the whites but among their [the Indians'] own chiefs and headmen as well."[3] For the other, we are indebted to Paul W. Gates, who in the centennial year of the Kansas-Nebraska Act wrote that Kansas Territory was thrown open to settlement when not one acre of land from Missouri to the Continental Divide was legally open to sale, and perhaps more important, "when there was emerging the most complex and confusing array of policies affecting the distribution of public lands and the transfer to white ownership of Indian land-rights that has ever emerged in the continental United States, save perhaps Oklahoma." The sorry result was that "land, slavery, plunder and patronage combined" became the order of the day, which explains why, unlike nearby Nebraska and other Indian country states, the Kansas struggle was so devastating for Indians and the future of Indian country.[4]

In this respect the personal attacks on Commissioner Manypenny, including his having been slurred as a "Rascally Copperhead" by a squatter who believed he had been cheated out of an Indian country claim by Manypenny,[5] are well worth recalling. In one of the commissioner's more vitriolic responses, which was reprinted in the national press, he wrote to Congressman Benton, venting his frustration and anger over his supposed inability to do anything about the worsening situation in Indian country:

> Now sir, led on by you, I defy them all. If they can strike another blow, let them level it; if they can invent another slander, let them utter it. I dare their worst efforts, and hold their conduct, and yours, sir, in unreserved contempt. . . . But were I unstained by a solitary human being, so long as I am entrusted with the administration of Indian affairs *I will not* allow the Indians to be plundered of their money or lands. . . . I will neither be frightened by personal violence nor coaxed by pleasant mannered men into aiding or sanctioning their schemes. . . . I have ceased to be surprised at anything that happens in Indian affairs. . . . We are in strange times.[6]

This was not the harangue of a mindless political crank but rather the unabashed assertion of an esteemed but much maligned public official convinced that the intrusion and demise of a place called Indian country dating back to the days of President Jackson were moving forward with full force on the prairie-plains west of Missouri.[7] "Already the white population is occupying the lands between and adjacent to the Indian reservations," wrote Manypenny in his annual report of 1854, "and at no distant day, all the country immediately to the west of the reserves, which is worth taking, will have been taken up." He hoped, however, that all was not lost for the first residents of the continent. "On the ground they now occupy the crisis must be met and their future determined. . . . Extermination might be their fate," he continued, "but not of necessity. By a union of good influences, and a proper effort they may, and will be saved, and their complete civilization effected."[8]

With this pronouncement Commissioner Manypenny backed off from his tormentors, perhaps from personal frustration or a true belief in the "union of good influences" or a combination of the two. But the fundamental issue raised by the Benton-Manypenny controversy would not go away. It was land, as we have seen, an immense amount of land. The ceded land disputed by Benton and Manypenny amounted to more than 80 percent of the present state of Kansas alone. Absent legal alterations by treaty or statute prior to the creation of Indian country under the 1834 law, was that area simply space, as Thomas McKenney had advised Secretary Barbour in 1825, or merely vacant land as Secretary Cass had called it in 1834?[9] A temporary or perhaps permanent sanctuary for displaced Indians not wanted in the East? Or had it become, pure and simple, part of the public domain when the 1825 and 1833 cession treaties were proclaimed and therefore open to settlement by *both* Indians and non-Indians in 1834?

All things considered, the ceded land was vacant only if by "vacant" is meant the absence of any human habitation whatsoever, Indian or non-Indian. It was a blatant rejection of much evidence that Indians and their non-Indian traders had been in the trans-Missouri

West for well over a century. And the ceded land was a refuge for displaced Indians early on, as evidenced by the removal of the Cape Girardeau Shawnees to a tract on the Kansas River west of Missouri nine years prior to 1834 and the removal of the several bands of Ottawas to a reservation in future Indian country.[10]

It is with the public domain option, therefore, where the basic problem lay. The 1825 Osage and Kansa cession treaties, as we have seen, were signed in St. Louis on June 2 and 3 respectively. If, in fact, the ceded land thereby became part of the public domain, why did the government negotiate the Santa Fe Trail rights-of-way treaties with the same tribes more than two months later: with the Osages on August 10, 1825, and with the Kansas on August 16? The least convincing explanation is that an unfortunate lack of communication resulted in the government's failure to understand that the June treaties rendered the August treaties unnecessary; or, perhaps, that because the two cession treaties were not officially proclaimed law until December 30, 1825, the August treaties were necessary for the promotion and growth of the Santa Fe trade in the meantime.

But as we have seen,[11] Fort Osage Factor George C. Sibley was in regular communication with his superiors in St. Louis and in attendance at all four of the 1825 parleys in the field, and was therefore privy to the details of the Santa Fe Trail treaties. Certainly there was no reason for Sibley or anyone else in the Indian Office to believe that the Senate would reject land cession agreements that played so directly into the government's emerging removal plan. A more reasonable explanation, then, is that the Santa Fe treaties were less important in terms of securing rights-of-way than in obtaining guarantees for a safe and unmolested non-Indian presence in future Indian country, or as both the Osage and Kansa agreements stated, "forever free for the use of the citizens of the United States, and of the Republic of Mexico."[12]

Whether Manypenny actually understood or was even aware of

what the Santa Fe treaties meant for the future of Indian country cannot be determined with certainty from the records of the Indian Office. What can be gleaned from his own writing is that he viewed the 1825 land cession treaties as a strong foundation upon which the emigrant Indians would be able to build permanent homes in the West,[13] and that the overland road to Mexico was important more for its economic and political impact on Missouri and the American frontier economy than a threat to the well-being of an Indian country of the future.

Armed with funds that had only recently been provided by Congress for breaking the Indian barrier, Manypenny moved forward with his self-proclaimed "proper effort."[14] Between March 15 and June 5, 1854, in his Washington office far removed from an increasingly unstable Indian country—a place the national press was beginning to call "Bleeding Kansas"—he concluded cession treaties with nine Indian country tribes, thereby placing into motion the legal machinery that would hasten the compression of Indian land, provide rights-of-way and land to railroad corporations across the entire reach of Indian country, and clear title to millions of acres of land for white farmers, town promoters, and land speculators soon to take up residence there. Some of the intruders themselves were exploited, as demonstrated by an 1857 report that Ely Moore, registrar at the Lecompton land office near present-day Topeka, had issued bogus preemption certificates that became objects of speculation on the nearby Miami reservation.[15] Over the next two decades nearly 13,000,000 acres of Indian country land west of Missouri passed directly from tribal ownership to land and railroad companies, missionary societies, and individuals without becoming part of the public domain or subject to congressional control. Indeed, as Manypenny had represented the existence of Indian country as a "dead letter" only a few months earlier,[16] it may not be too much to suggest that the Manypenny treaties were self-fulfilling prophecies.

Nevertheless, the advent of Kansas Territory was no more the main culprit in the decline of Indian country than the land cession and right-of-way treaties of 1825 and 1833, or the failure of the Western Territory bill in 1834, or the overland road to Mexico in 1825 and to Oregon and California a decade later, or the Platte Purchase of 1836, or the Benton-Manypenny map war of 1853. Although the decline and fall was a complex and cumulative development, its foundation was a voracious non-Indian demand for land promised to Indians, a demand that gave rise to unpleasant questions whose answers, with few exceptions, pulled at cross purposes and hence were difficult to resolve in the best interests of the Indians. Who, for example, would have the land, and for what purpose? By what means? And how would it affect the people to whom it was promised but who in the end were denied it? It is worth remembering also that the Indian country of 1834 was as much a place for controlling human behavior and modifying culture as it was a physical space simply to be occupied by a displaced people in need of security and the means of survival.

The alteration of old treaties by new laws and administrative tactics not generally understood by most Indians also contributed to the demise of Indian country, especially with regard to laws dealing with the production, distribution, and consumption of alcohol by Indians (and non-Indians) in Indian country. Commenting on the seemingly endless statutory revisions affecting the meaning of "in the Indian country," a federal judge in frontier Kansas concluded, "Whether selling a drink of liquor to an Indian who crossed the border for that purpose would be introducing liquor into the Indian country is a question in metaphysics too abstruse for me to solve, until driven to it by dire necessity."[17] Another official, obviously distressed by the blatantly illegal consumption of alcohol in Indian country, went as far as to recommend that Congress extend the trade and intercourse laws dealing with alcohol over all public lands contiguous to Indian country. "A jurisdiction of this nature," wrote Minnesota Territorial Governor Alexander Ramsey in 1850, "is essential to the safety of the Indian."[18] His recommendation, of course, fell on deaf ears.

Today, under authority of the U.S. Supreme Court,[19] Indian country is what and where Congress decides. It can be a high-rise casino encompassing a city block across the street from a private shopping mall. It can be a convenience store and service station complex along a federal or state highway. It can be a minuscule plot of sand required for a gas well platform in the middle of a stream, or it can be a vast underground oil deposit held in trust for the allotees of surface reservation land.[20] Or it can be acres and acres of sparsely inhabited tribal grazing land adjacent to small fee-simple truck farms made productive by Indian country water from a distant stream. In sum, Indian country today is a real and powerful force in the lives of many Indians, perhaps the majority. It is, with a few essentially procedural exceptions:

(a) all land within the limits of any Indian reservation under the jurisdiction of the United States Government, notwithstanding the issuance of any patent, and, including rights-of-way running through the reservations, (b) all dependent Indian communities within the borders of the United States whether within the original or subsequently acquired territory thereof, and whether within or without the limits of a state, and (c) all Indian allotments, the Indian titles to which have not been extinguished, including rights-of-way running through the same.[21]

But as we have seen, that was not always so. That the establishment of Indian country in 1834 was ineffectual and a failure from the beginning should come as no great surprise. Contrary to promises and declarations to the Indians of good and even better times to come, the prairie-plains west of Missouri and Iowa were attractive to non-Indians who displayed little or no sympathy for the idea, let alone the reality, of Indian residence and improvement in a place they themselves coveted. In fact the invasion of Indian country was well under way as early as 1825, and by 1854, when the floodgates of white settlement were finally opened, the government's safe haven for Indians was as illusory as it had been from the start.

Notes

Chapter One. Looking Backward

1 Francis Paul Prucha, *American Indian Policy in the Formative Years: The Trade and Intercourse Acts, 1790–1834* (Cambridge, MA: Harvard University Press, 1962), 274.

2 Ibid.

3 *U.S. Statutes at Large* 2 (1802): 139.

4 Prucha, *American Indian Policy,* 3.

5 *U.S. Statutes at Large* 4 (1834): 729.

6 Prucha, *American Indian Policy;* Ronald N. Satz, *American Indian Policy in the Jacksonian Era* (Lincoln: University of Nebraska Press, 1975). See also Francis Paul Prucha, *The Great Father: The United States Government and the American Indians* (Lincoln: University of Nebraska Press, 1984), vol. 1, chap. 11.

7 *U.S. Statutes at Large* 4 (1834): 729.

8 Vine Deloria, Jr., *Custer Died for Your Sins: An Indian Manifesto* (New York: Macmillan, 1969), 78.

9 Donald L. Fixico, *The Invasion of Indian Country: American Capitalism and Tribal Natural Resources* (Niwot: University Press of Colorado, 1998), 181.

10 Prucha, *American Indian Policy,* 261–262.

11 James P. Ronda, "'We Have a Country': Race, Geography, and the Invention of Indian Territory," *Journal of the Early Republic* 19, no. 3 (Fall 1999): 739–740.

12 *American State Papers, 2, Indian Affairs,* 2: 123–124.

13 Ibid.

14 Jefferson to Gates, July 11, 1803, Paul Leicester Ford, ed., *The Works of Thomas Jefferson* (New York: G. P. Putnam's Sons, 1905), 10: 12–14.

15 Jefferson to Dickinson, August 9, 1803, ibid., 29–30.

16 Jefferson to Breckenridge, August 11, 1803, ibid., 6–7.

17 Bernard Sheehan, *Seeds of Extinction: Jeffersonian Philanthropy and the American Indian* (New York: W. W. Norton, 1974), 245.

18 Drafts of an Amendment to the Constitution, July, 1803, Ford, *Works of Thomas Jefferson,* 10: 8–11.

19 Jefferson to Knox, August 10, 1791, cited in *Niles' Weekly Register* 44, August 10, 1832, p. 387.

20 James P. Ronda, *Lewis and Clark among the Indians* (Lincoln: University of Nebraska Press, 1984), 253.

21 *American State Papers*, 2, *Indian Affairs*, 2: 123–124.

22 James D. Richardson, comp., *A Compilation of the Messages and Papers of the Presidents, 1789–1897* (Washington, DC: Government Printing Office, 1896–1899), 2: 585; 2: 850; 3: 1021.

23 *U.S. Statutes at Large* 4 (1830): 411–412; Prucha, *American Indian Policy,* 239–244.

24 *U.S. Statutes at Large* 4 (1830): 411–412.

25 *U.S. Statutes at Large* 10 (1853): 238–239.

26 Ibid.

27 H. Craig Miner and William E. Unrau, *The End of Indian Kansas: A Study of Cultural Revolution, 1854–1871* (Lawrence: Regents Press of Kansas, 1978), 139.

28 David J. Wishart, *An Unspeakable Sadness: The Dispossession of the Nebraska Indians* (Lincoln: University of Nebraska Press, 1994), 188.

29 Quish-Queh-Leh to President of the United States, November 20, 1835, *Senate Document* no. 348, 24-1, serial 283, 348; *Niles' Weekly Register* 45 (August 31, 1833), 10–11.

30 Statement of R. S. Elliott, former Council Bluffs Subagent, on behalf of a Potawatomi delegation, November 12, 1845, Journal of the Proceedings of the Board of Commissioners Appointed by Letter of the Secretary of War, November 3, 1845, Ratified Treaties, 1838–1853, Record Group 75, Target 494, Roll 4, National Archives and Records Administration.

31 George W. Manypenny, *Our Indian Wards* (1880; repr., New York: Da Capo Press, 1972), 121–122.

32 Robert M. Kvasnicka, "George W. Manypenny," in Robert M. Kvasnicka and Herman J. Viola, eds., *The Commissioners of Indian Affairs, 1824–1977* (Lincoln: University of Nebraska Press, 1979), 62.

33 Manypenny, *Our Indian Wards,* 121.

34 Prucha, *American Indian Policy,* 275.

35 Satz, *American Indian Policy*, 294.

36 Robert A. Trennert, Jr., *Alternative to Extinction: Federal Indian Policy and the Beginnings of the Reservation System, 1846–51* (Philadelphia: Temple University Press, 1975), 193–194, 197.

37 Rev. C. G. Boynton and T. B. Mason, *A Journey through Kansas; with Sketches of Nebraska: Describing the Country, Climate, Soil, Minerals, Manufacturing, and Other Resources. The Results of a Tour in the Autumn of 1854* (Cincinnati: Moore, Wilstach, Keys, 1855), 23.

38 John C. McCoy to George W. Manypenny, October 10, 1855, Letters Received by the Office of Indian Affairs, Record Group 75, Microfilm 234, Shawnee Agency, Roll 809, National Archives and Records Administration.

39 William Phillips, *The Conquest of Kansas, by Missouri and Her Allies* (Boston: Phillips, Sampson, 1856), 18.

40 *National Intelligencer*, June 25, 1857.

41 Ronda, "'We Have a Country,'" 746.

42 *Bates v. Clark*, 95 U.S. 204 (1877).

43 Ibid., 209.

44 Ibid., 207.

45 Ibid., 204.

46 See, for example, Kevin Abing, "Before Bleeding Kansas: Christian Missionaries, Slavery, and the Shawnee Indians in Pre-Territorial Kansas, 1844–1854," *Kansas History: A Journal of the Central Plains* 24, no. 1 (Spring 2001): 54–70. On October 30, 1847, Richard Mendenall wrote a letter from the Shawnee Friends Mission in Indian country (just across the line from Westport, Missouri, in present Johnson County, Kansas), titled "The existence of slavery in this Territory, contrary to the restrictions of the Missouri Compromise." In the letter, which was printed in the *National Era* (Washington) on December 23, 1847, Mendenall charged that "it is the white men in the service of the Government of the United States, and missionaries, that have introduced slavery here." Shawnee Chief Joseph Parks owned a number of slaves, reported Mendenall, and missionaries in charge of the Shawnee Methodist Mission, operated by the Methodist Episcopal Church, South, had "half a dozen or more slaves." Many of the Indians were opposed to slavery in Indian country, said Mendenall, "but there are others who, no doubt, would own slaves if they were able to buy them." Quoted in Louise Barry, comp., *The Beginning of the West: Annals of the Kansas Gateway to the American West, 1540–1854* (Topeka: Kansas State Historical Society, 1972), 723.

47 Lynn Hudson Parsons, "'A Perpetual Harrow upon My Feelings': John Quincy Adams and the American Indian," *New England Quarterly* 46, no. 3 (September 1973): 339–340.

48 Ibid., 345–346.

49 Ibid., 378.

Chapter Two. Reconnaissance

1 Bernard DeVoto, *The Year of Decision, 1846* (Cambridge, MA: Riverside Press, 1942), 4.

2 Ibid.

3 The literature on Indian removal is extensive, including individual volumes dealing with the removal experiences of specific tribes. The best summary is in Francis Paul Prucha, *The Great Father, The United States Government and the American Indian* (Lincoln: University of Nebraska Press, 1984), 2: 179–269.

4 Charles J. Kappler, comp., *Indian Affairs: Laws and Treaties* (Washington: Government Printing Office, 1904), 2: 222; Charles C. Royce, *Indian Land Cessions in the United States,* Eighteenth Annual Report of the Bureau of American Ethnology, 1896–1897, pt. 2 (Washington, DC: Government Printing Office, 1899), Kansas Map 1.

5 Kappler, *Treaties,* 2: 552–554.

6 Ibid., 557–560.

7 Edwin Bryant, *What I Saw in California* (1848; repr. with an introduction by Thomas D. Clark, Lincoln: University of Nebraska Press, 1985), 19, 55–56.

8 Ibid., 61.

9 Heinrich Lienhard, *From St. Louis to Sutter's Fort, 1846,* trans. Edwin G. and Elisabeth K. Gudde (Norman: University of Oklahoma Press, 1961), 18.

10 *Gazette* (St. Joseph, Missouri), July 18, 1845, cited in John D. Unruh, Jr., *The Plains Across: The Overland Emigrants and the Trans-Mississippi West, 1840–1860* (Urbana: University of Illinois Press, 1979), 56–57.

11 Entry for April 22, 1847, Norton Jacob Diary, Richard H. Jackson, ed., *The Mormon Role in the Settlement of the West* (Provo, Utah: Brigham Young University Press, 1978), 10.

12 Entry for June 26, 1847, Levi Jackman Journal, ibid., 13.

13 Entry for August 15, 1849, Martha Heywood Diary, ibid., 10–11.

14 Louise Barry, comp., *The Beginning of the West: Annals of the Kansas Gateway to the American West, 1540–1854* (Topeka: Kansas State Historical Society, 1972), 576.

15 Unruh, *The Plains Across,* 84–85, tables 2 and 3.

16 Leo E. Oliva, *Soldiers on the Santa Fe Trail* (Norman: University of Oklahoma Press, 1967), 55.

17 Barry, *The Beginning of the West,* 589.

18 Robert A. Trennert, Jr., *Alternative to Extinction: Federal Indian Policy and the Beginnings of the Reservation System, 1846–51* (Philadelphia: Temple University Press, 1975), 18–19.

19 Ibid., 29.

20 William H. Goetzmann, *Exploration and Empire: The Explorer and the Scientist in the Winning of the American West* (New York: Alfred A. Knopf, 1966), 51, 62, 64.

21 Meriwether Lewis to his mother (Lucy Marks), March 31, 1805, Reuben Gold Thwaites, ed., *Original Journals of the Lewis and Clark Expedition, 1804–1806* (New York: Dodd, Mead, 1904–05): 7: 310–11. See also James P. Ronda, *Finding the West: Explorations with Lewis and Clark* (Albuquerque: University of New Mexico Press, 2001), 66–69.

22 Jervis Cutler, *A Topographical Description of the State of Ohio, Indiana Territory, and Louisiana . . . to Which Is Added an Interesting Journal of Mr. Charles Le Raye While Captive with the Sioux Nation on the Waters of the Missouri River* (Boston: Charles Williams–J. Belcher Printer, 1812), 158, 162, 165–166.

23 *Eclectic Review* (London), 7 (April 1811), cited in Archer Butler Hulbert, ed., *Southwest on the Turquoise Trail: The First Diaries on the Road to Santa Fe* (Colorado Springs: Stewart Commission of Colorado College, 1933; Denver: Denver Public Library, 1933), 2–3.

24 Ibid., 5.

25 Goetzmann, *Exploration and Empire,* xii–xiii.

26 John Bradbury, *Travels in the Interior of America in the Years 1809, 1810, and 1811* (1817; repr., Readex Microprint, 1966), 5: 242–244, 272.

27 Henry Marie Brackenridge, *Views of Louisiana Together with a Journal of a Voyage up the Missouri River, in 1811* (1814; repr., Chicago: Quadrangle Books, 1962), 29, 33–34.

28 Thomas D. Isern, ed., "Exploration and Diplomacy: George Champlin Sibley's Report to William Clark," *Missouri Historical Review* 73, no. 1 (October 1978): 85–86.

29 Clark to Secretary of War, June 1, 1807, Clarence E. Carter, comp. and ed., *The Territorial Papers of the United States* (Washington, DC: Government Printing Office, 1934–56): 14: 122–123; Isern, "Exploration and Diplomacy," 86, 97–99.

30 Isern, "Exploration and Diplomacy," 87–102.

31 Ibid., 87–96.

32 Kappler, *Treaties* 2: 214–217.

33 Clark to James Barbour, Secretary of War, June 11, 1825, *American State Papers, 2, Indian Affairs* 2: 591–592.

34 For example, see *Niles' Weekly Register*, February 24, 1824, p. 357, which confirmed certain desert phenomena reported by members of Long's party, including the flow of the Platte and Arkansas rivers through a "dreary waste."

35 August Storrs to Senator Thomas Hart Benton, January 17, 1825, under the title "Collocation of the Indians," in ibid., 407.

36 Ibid.

37 Francis Paul Prucha, "Indian Removal and the Great American Desert," *Indiana Magazine of History* 59, no. 4 (December 1963): 322. See also James C. Malin, *The Grassland of North America, Prolegomena to Its History with Addenda and Postscript* (Gloucester, MA: Peter Smith, 1967), 442–443; Martin J. Bowden, "The Perception of the Western Interior of the United States, 1800–1870: A Problem in Historical Geosophy," *Proceedings of the Association of American Geographers* 1 (1969): 16–21; and Merle Paul Lawson, *The Climate of the Great American Desert: Reconstruction of the Climate of Western Interior United States, 1800–1850* (Lincoln: University of Nebraska Press, 1974), 1–32, 95.

38 Isaac McCoy to Secretary of War John H. Eaton, September 30, 1830, and April n.d., 1832, Correspondence on the Subject of the Emigration of Indians between the 30th of November and 27th of December, 1833, with Abstracts of Expenditures by Disbursing Agents in the Removal and Subsistence of Indians, &c., &c., 2, *Senate Executive Document*, no. 512, 23-1, serial 245, 173, 431–432, 436.

39 Henry Leavitt Ellsworth, *Washington Irving on the Prairie or a Narrative of a Tour of the Southwest in the Year 1832*, ed. Stanley T. Williams and Barbara D. Simpson (New York: American Book, 1937), 60–61.

40 McCoy to Lewis Cass, February 1, 1832, Country for Indians West of the Mississippi, *House Document* no. 172, 22-1, serial 219, 10–11. Whether McCoy was aware of the Supreme Court's ruling in *Johnson and Graham's Lessee v. McIntosh*, 8 Wheaton 592 (1823), which held that the ultimate title to Indian land was vested in the United States, is not known.

41 Francis Paul Prucha, *The Great Father* 1: 304.

42 William E. Unrau, "George C. Sibley's Plea for the 'Garden of Missouri' in 1824," *Missouri Historical Society Bulletin* 17, no. 1 (October 1970): 5.

43 Memorandum of a preliminary arrangement (for the purchase and sale of lands) made on the 20th day of September 1818 at Fort Osage between G. C. Sibley Superintendent of Indian affairs for the U. States acting in this manner under instructions from His Execy. Governor Clark on the one part and the chiefs and head men of the Kansas nation on the other part, George C. Sibley Papers, Missouri Historical Society; Unrau, "George C. Sibley's Plea," 6–7.

44 Sibley to Barton, January 10, 1824, Sibley Papers.

Chapter Three. Preparing the Way

1 Jesse H. Leavenworth to Dennis N. Cooley, May 8, 1866, Letters Received by the Office of Indian Affairs, Record Group 75, Microfilm 234, Kiowa-Comanche Agency, Roll 375, National Archives and Records Administration.

2 William E. Unrau, "The Civil War Career of Jesse Henry Leavenworth," *Montana: The Magazine of Western History* 12, no. 2 (Spring 1961): 74–82; Carolyn Thomas Foreman, "Colonel Jesse Henry Leavenworth," *Chronicles of Oklahoma* 13, no. 1 (March 1933): 14–15; *Rocky Mountain News* (Denver), February 6, 1861; Thomas M. Marshall, ed., "Minutes of the Eureka District," *Early Records of Gilpin County, Colorado, 1859–1861* (Denver: W. F. Robinson, 1920), 81, 96, 99; Judge Advocate General's Report (typed copy), Washington, February 18, 1864, Second Colorado Regiment Veterans Papers, Manuscript Division, State Historical Society of Colorado.

3 Leavenworth to Cooley, May 8, 1866.

4 Charles J. Kappler, comp., *Indian Affairs: Laws and Treaties* (Washington, DC: Government Printing Office, 1904), 2: 892–895.

5 *Niles' Weekly Register*, September 6, 1834, p. 10. As early as 1818, the same paper speculated on some possibilities for at least some of this "unappropriated" land in the West, possibilities that appeared to anticipate the pull of Manifest Destiny of a later date: "Those who can look back 50 years, may form some idea of what the next will do for the United States—and such is the thirst for diving into the interior, that if any system is to be adopted to preserve the Indians, it ought to be adopted at once, to make it efficient. A little while, and we shall be treating for land about the headsprings of the Mississippi, and in a few years we might hear of a national road winding through the passes of the Rocky Mountains, the only *land* carriage between the city of New York and a great city built at the mouth of the Columbia." Ibid., November 14, 1818.

6 Francis Paul Prucha, *American Indian Policy in the Formative Years: The Trade and Intercourse Acts, 1790–1834* (Cambridge, MA: Harvard University Press, 1962), 269–273.

7 Louise Barry, comp., *The Beginning of the West: Annals of the Kansas Gateway to the American West, 1540–1854* (Topeka: Kansas State Historical Society, 1972), 97, 105; William H. Goetzmann, *Exploration and Empire: The Explorer and the Scientist in the Winning of the American West* (New York: Alfred A. Knopf, 1966), 66; *U.S. Statutes at Large* 4 (1825): 100–101.

8 Kappler, *Treaties*, 2: 246–250.

9 Buford Rowland, ed., "Report of the Commissioners on the Road from Missouri to New Mexico, October 27 [1825]," *New Mexico Historical Review* 14,

no. 3 (July 1939): 225–226; "Field Notes of Joseph C. Brown, United States Surveying Expedition, 1825–1827," in Archer Butler Hulbert, ed., *Southwest on the Turquoise Trail: The First Diaries on the Road to Santa Fe*, vol. 2, *Overland to the Pacific* (Colorado Springs and Denver: Stewart Commission of Colorado College and the Denver Public Library, 1933), 105, 107, 123, 142.

10 Rowland, "Report of the Commissioners," 217n15.

11 Clark to James Barbour, June 11, 1825, Documents Relating to the Negotiation of Ratified and Unratified Treaties with the Various Tribes of Indians, 1801–69, Introduction and Ratified Treaties, 1801–26, Record Group 75, Target 494, Roll 1, National Archives and Records Administration.

12 Barry, *The Beginning of the West*, 166.

13 Kappler, *Treaties*, 2: 225, 249–250; Paul Wilhelm, Duke of Wuerttenberg, "First Journey to North America in the Years 1822–1824," trans. William G. Beck, *South Dakota Historical Collections* 19 (1938): 166–167; William E. Unrau, *Mixed-Bloods and Tribal Dissolution: Charles Curtis and the Quest for Indian Identity* (Lawrence: University Press of Kansas, 1989), 26–27, 30.

14 Kappler, *Treaties*, 2: 225, 248–249; Memorandum of a preliminary arrangement . . . of September 1818, Sibley Papers; William E. Unrau, "George C. Sibley's Plea for the 'Garden of Missouri' in 1824," *Missouri Historical Society Bulletin* 17, no. 1 (October 1970), 8.

15 Thomas McKenney to James Barbour, November 30, 1825, Documents Accompanying the President's Message to Congress, December 6, 1825, Office of Indian Affairs, November 30, 1825, *House Document* no. 1, 19-1, serial 131, 91.

16 Quish-Qeh-Leh to President of the United States, November 20, 1835, *Senate Document* no. 384, 24-1, serial 283, 348.

17 Clark to James Barbour, June 11, 1825, Documents Relating to the Negotiation of Ratified and Unratified Treaties with the Various Tribes of Indians, 1801–69, Introduction and Ratified Treaties, 1801–26, Record Group 75, Target 494, Roll 1, National Archives and Records Administration.

18 *U.S. Statutes at Large* 4 (1825) 100–101.

19 James D. Richardson, comp., *A Compilation of the Messages and Papers of the Presidents, 1789–1897* (Washington, DC: Government Printing Office, 1896–1899), 2: 585.

20 Ibid., 849–859.

21 Prucha, *American Indian Policy*, 227.

22 Michael E. Green, *The Politics of Indian Removal: Creek Government and Society in Crisis* (Lincoln, University of Nebraska Press, 1982), 73, 787–789.

23 *"Proposition to Extinguish Indian Title to Lands in Missouri, Communicated to the Senate, May 14, 1824,"* American State Papers, 2, Indian Affairs, 2: 512.

24 Kappler, *Treaties*, 2: 214–215.

25 Ibid., 215.

26 Clark to Barbour, June 11, 1825, Documents Relating to the Negotiation of Ratified and Unratified Treaties with the Various Tribes of Indians, 1801–69, Introduction and Ratified Treaties, 1801–26, Record Group 75, Target 494, Roll 1, National Archives and Records Administration.

27 *U.S. Statutes at Large* 3 (1819): 516–517.

28 For example, in the Kansa treaty of 1846, which ceded an additional 2,000,000 acres of land in Indian country, Article 2 provided that "four hundred dollars shall be paid to the Missionary Society of the Methodist Episcopal Church for their improvements on the [2,000,000 acres of] land ceded in the first article." Sixteen years later, Article 2 of the 1862 Kansa treaty provided that "the Kansa tribe of Indians, being desirous of making a suitable expression of the obligations the said tribe are under to Thomas S. Huffaker, hereby authorize and request the Secretary of the Interior to convey to the said Thomas S. Huffaker as [Methodist Episcopal] missionary, teacher, and friendly counselor of said tribe of Indians the half-section of land on which he has resided and improved and cultivated since the year A.D. 1851 . . . at a rate not less that one dollar and seventy- five cents an acre." Kappler, *Treaties,* 2: 553, 829. In the spring of 1863 Special Commissioner Edward Wolcott advised the Indian Office that the half-section in question "was easily worth $20 per acre." See William E. Unrau, *The Kansa Indians: A History of the Wind People, 1673–1873* (Norman: University of Oklahoma Press, 1971), 192; and Paul Wallace Gates, *Fifty Million Acres: Conflicts over Kansas Land Policy, 1854–1890* (Ithaca, NY: Cornell University Press, 1954), 7–8, 50.

29 "Mission to the Osages," *Missionary Herald* 17 (January 1821): 25–26.

30 Ibid., 26; "Mission to the Great Osages," *Missionary Herald* 18 (January 1822): 30–31; "Great Osage Mission," *Missionary Herald* 19 (July 1823): 214–215.

31 Barry, *Beginning of the West,* 117; "The Osages," *Missionary Herald* 22 (January 1826): 5–6. See also Willard H. Rollings, *The Osage: An Ethnohistorical Study of Hegemony on the Prairie-Plains* (Columbia: University of Missouri Press, 1992), 260–261; and John Joseph Mathews, *The Osages: Children of the Middle Waters* (Norman: University of Oklahoma Press, 1961), 464.

32 Kevin B. Ast, "Divided We Stand: Osage Leadership before Removal" (M.A. thesis, Wichita State University, 1991), 45–46.

33 Ibid., 46–47; Barry, *Beginning of the West,* 136, 158.

34 Commissioner Denver's Talk with Kaw Indians in Washington, July 22, 1857, Letters Received by the Office of Indian Affairs, Record Group 75, Microfilm 234, Kansas Agency, Roll 365, National Archives and Records Administration.

35 Mathews, *The Osages,* 464.

36 Kappler, *Treaties,* 2: 599.

37 Ibid., 613–614. An early mission school superintendent of the religious body awarded the 640 acres of Omaha land in the 1854 treaty told the tribe in 1846 that the missionaries had come "to tell them how to live and how to die" and implied that the Omahas would pass out of existence if they refused to accept the white man's God. See Judith A. Boughter, *Betraying the Omaha Nation, 1790–1916* (Norman: University of Oklahoma Press, 1998), 83–84.

38 In 1849, for example, Baptist missionary-teacher Jotham Meeker, from his Indian country station not far from the site of the defunct UFMS Neosho mission dating back to mid-1820s, reported the conversion of more than half of the removed Ottawa tribe. Four hundred acres of reservation land were under cultivation, reported Meeker, and numerous cattle and hogs were supplementing the annual $2,600 issued by the government to the Baptists for tribal improvement. See George A. Schultz, *An Indian Canaan: Isaac McCoy and the Vision of an Indian State* (Norman: University of Oklahoma Press, 1972), 198; and William E. Unrau and H. Craig Miner, *Tribal Dispossession and the Ottawa Indian University Fraud* (Norman: University of Oklahoma Press, 1985), 66.

39 Kappler, *Treaties,* 2: 236.

40 Carl G. Klopfenstein, "Westward Ho: Removal of the Ohio Shawnees, 1832–1833," *Bulletin of the Historical and Philosophical Society of Ohio* 15 (January 1957): 3–31.

41 Gary N. Damron, "The Friends Missionary Establishment among the Shawnee Indians in Kansas" (M.A. thesis, Wichita State University, 1985), 37–42; Martha B. Caldwell, ed., *Annals of the Shawnee Methodist Mission and Indian Manual Labor School* (Topeka: Kansas State Historical Society, 1930), 7–13.

42 Marston G. Clark to General William Clark, October 7, 1834, Letters Received by the Office of Indian Affairs, Record Group 75, Microfilm 234, Fort Leavenworth Agency, Roll 302, National Archives and Records Administration.

43 William Clark to Elbert Herring, April 8, 1835, ibid.

44 Marston G. Clark to Lewis Cass, February 27, 1835, ibid.

45 Roger L. Nichols, *General Henry Atkinson, A Western Military Career* (Norman: University of Oklahoma Press, 1965), 90–109; Letter of the Sec. of War, Transmitting the Information Required by a Resolution of the House of Representatives of the 1st Inst., Respecting the Movements of the Expedition which lately Ascended the Missouri River, &c, March 6, 1826, *House Document* no. 117, 19-1, serial 136, 15–16.

46 Robert W. Frazer, *Forts of the West: Military Forts and Presidios and Posts Commonly Called Forts West of the Mississippi River to 1898* (Norman: University of Oklahoma Press, 1965), 16–17, 67, 84–85, 119–120, 125.

47 Ibid., 56.

48 H. Craig Miner and William E. Unrau, *The End of Indian Kansas: A Study of Cultural Revolution, 1854–1871* (Lawrence: Regents Press of Kansas, 1978), 13–16.

49 *The Writings of Thomas Jefferson* (Washington: Thomas Jefferson Memorial Association, 1905), 16: 451–452.

50 Robert W. McCluggage, "The Senate and Indian Land Titles, 1800–1825," *Western Historical Quarterly* 1, no. 4 (October 1970): 415–425.

51 William Clark to John C. Calhoun, February 6, 1818, *American State Papers, 2, Indian Affairs,* 2: 173.

52 John C. Calhoun to William Clark, May 8, 1818, ibid., 174.

53 McCluggage, "The Senate and Indian Land Titles," 418–420; Paul W. Gates, "Indian Allotments Preceding the Dawes Act," in John G. Clark, ed., *The Frontier Challenge: Responses to the Trans-Mississippi West* (Lawrence: University Press of Kansas, 1971), 145–152.

54 Kappler, *Treaties,* 2: 218–219, 223.

55 See, for example, the Act of July 17, 1862, *U.S. Statutes at Large* 12 (1862): 628, which confirmed vested titles to the 640-acre plots in the original "half-breed" reservees and their heirs.

56 Clark to James Barbour, June 11, Documents Relating to the Negotiation of Ratified and Unratified Treaties with the Various Tribes of Indians, 1801–69, Introduction and Ratified Treaties, 1801–26, Record Group 75, Target 494, Roll 1, National Archives and Records Administration.

Chapter Four. Promise

1 William Clark to James Barbour, March 1, 1826, *American State Papers, 2, Indian Affairs,* 2: 654.

2 Jerome O. Steffan, *William Clark: Jeffersonian Man on the Frontier* (Norman: University of Oklahoma Press, 1977), 7–8.

3 Francis Paul Prucha, *American Indian Policy in the Formative Years: The Trade and Intercourse Acts, 1790–1834* (Cambridge, MA: Harvard University Press, 1962), 250–251.

4 Peter B. Porter to Lewis Cass, July 28, 1828, cited in ibid., 252.

5 Clark to Porter, August 27, 1828, cited in Steffan, *William Clark,* 144.

6 Willard Carl Klunder, *Lewis Cass and the Politics of Moderation* (Kent, OH: Kent State University Press, 1996), 47, 49–50. See also Francis Paul Prucha, *Lewis Cass and American Indian Policy* (Detroit: Wayne State University Press, 1967); and Elizabeth Gasser Brown, "Lewis Cass and the American Indian," *Michigan History* 37 (September 1953): 294–297.

7 *Niles' Weekly Register,* December 2, 1826, p. 218.

8 Ibid.

9 *U.S. Statutes at Large* 4 (1830): 411–412.

10 Charles J. Kappler, comp., *Indian Affairs: Laws and Treaties* (Washington, DC: Government Printing Office, 1904), 2: 258–260.

11 Louise Barry, comp., *The Beginning of the West: Annals of the Kansas Gateway to the American West, 1540–1854* (Topeka: Kansas State Historical Society, 1972), 169–172.

12 John D. Unruh, Jr., *The Plains Across: The Overland Emigrants and the Trans-Mississippi West, 1840–1860* (Urbana: University of Illinois Press, 1979), 128.

13 Peter B. Porter to President of the Senate, February 9, 1829, Report from the Secretary of War, in compliance with resolutions of the Senate of the 10th of December and 15th of January, 1829, relative to Indian Affairs, &c. &c., *Senate Document* no. 72, 20-2, serial 181, 1–2.

14 Ibid., 27.

15 *U.S. Statutes at Large* 2 (1802): 141.

16 Report from the Secretary of War, in compliance with resolutions of the Senate of the 10th of December and 15th of January, 1829, relative to Indian Affairs, &c. &c., *Senate Document* no. 72, 20-2, serial 181, 27.

17 Elbert Herring to Lewis Cass, November 19, 1831, *House Executive Document* no. 2, 23-1, serial 216, 175.

18 Kappler, *Treaties,* 2: 305–310.

19 Cited in Howard I. McCoy, "The Platte Purchase," *Missouri Historical Review* 32, no. 2 (January 1938): 131–132.

20 Report from the Secretary of War, in compliance with resolutions of the Senate of the 10th of December and 15th of January, 1829, relative to Indian Affairs, &c. &c., *Senate Document* no. 72, 20-2, serial 181, 31.

21 Report of the Secretary of War, November 21, 1831, *House Executive Document* no. 2, 22-1, serial 216, 30, 32–33.

22 James D. Richardson, comp., *A Compilation of the Messages and Papers of the Presidents, 1789–1897* (Washington, DC: Government Printing Office, 1896–1899), 3: 1117–1118.

23 *U.S. Statutes at Large* 4 (1832): 564.

24 Clark to Elbert Herring, December 3, 1831, Letters Received by the Office of Indian Affairs, Record Group 75, Microfilm 234, St. Louis Superintendency, Roll 749, National Archives and Records Administration.

25 Lewis Cass, "Remarks on the Policy and Practices of the United States and Great Britain in Their Treatment of the Indians," *North American Review* 24 (April 1827): 404.

26 *U.S. Statutes at Large* 3 (1822): 682–683.

27 P. L. Chouteau to Lewis Cass, September 19, 1832, Letters Received by the Office of Indian Affairs, Record Group 75, Microfilm 234, Osage Agency, Roll 631, National Archives and Records Administration.

28 Regulating the Indian Department, May 20, 1834, and Henry L. Ellsworth to Cass, May 13, 1834, *House Report* no. 474, 23-1, serial 263, 76, 79–83; Country for Indians West of the Mississippi. Letter to the Secretary of War, transmitting a copy of a report made by Isaac McCoy, upon the subject of the country reserved for the Indians west of the Mississippi, *House Document* no. 172, 22-1, serial 219, 13–14.

29 For Cass's correspondence during the period in question, see Records of the Office of the Secretary of War, Record Group 107, Microfilm 6, Letters Sent, Military Affairs, 1800–1861, Rolls 13 and 14, National Archives and Records Service.

30 Regulating the Indian Department, May 20, 1834, and Map of the Western Territory &c., *House Report* no. 474, 23-1, serial 263, 17–18.

31 Prucha, *American Indian Policy*, 270.

32 *Register of Debates in Congress*, 23-1 (June 25, 1834), 4779.

33 Ibid., 4763–4772.

34 Lynn Hudson Parsons, "'A Perpetual Harrow upon My Feelings': John Quincy Adams and the American Indian," *New England Quarterly* 46, no. 3 (September 1973): 344.

35 *Register of Debates in Congress*, 23-1 (June 25, 1834), 4769.

36 Ibid., 4770.

37 Ibid., 4776–4777.

38 Ibid., 4779.

39 *U.S. Statutes at Large* 4 (1834): 729.

40 Felix S. Cohen, *Handbook of Federal Indian Law* (Washington, DC: Government Printing Office, 1942), 5.

41 *U.S. Statutes at Large* 4 (1834): 729–734.

42 Barry, *Beginning of the West*, 256–257. See also George E. Hyde, *A Life of George Bent Written from His Letters*, ed. Savoie Lottinville (Norman: University of Oklahoma Press, 1967), 60–61.

43 William E. Unrau, *White Man's Wicked Water: The Alcohol Trade and Prohibition in Indian Country, 1802–1892* (Lawrence: University Press of Kansas, 1996), 33. On April 27, 1859, William Bent was appointed U.S. Indian agent for the Upper Arkansas Agency, which, in the late 1850s and early 1860s, was responsible for the Southern Cheyennes and Arapahos in present-day western Kansas and eastern Colorado. See Edward H. Hill, *The Office of Indian Affairs, 1824–1880: Historical Sketches* (New York: Clearwater Publishing, 1974), 183–184.

44 Unrau, *White Man's Wicked Water,* 42–43.

45 Cass to William Marshall, July 12, 1834, Documents Relating to the Negotiation of the Treaty of October 23, 1834, with the Miami Indians, Documents Relating to the Negotiation of Ratified and Unratified Treaties with the Various Tribes of Indians, 1801–69, Record Group 75, Target 494, Roll 3, National Archives and Records Administration.

46 Kappler, *Treaties,* 2: 425–428, 531–534.

47 Journal of the Proceedings of the Council held with the Miami Nation of Indians at the Fork of the Wabash, in the state of Indiana, by Governor George B. Porter of Michigan, General William Marshall of Indiana, and the Reverend J. F. Schermerhorn, Commissioners appointed by the President of the United States to negotiate with said Nation for the purchase of their lands, n.d., 1830, Letters Received by the Office of Indian Affairs, Record Group 75, Microfilm 234, Miami Agency, Roll 416, National Archives and Records Administration.

Chapter Five. Presence

1 Rev. Jedidiah Morse, *Report to the Secretary of War of the United States on Indian Affairs, Comprising a Narrative of a Tour Performed in the Summer of 1820* (New Haven, CT: S. Converse, 1822), 366–367, table 1.

2 William E. Unrau, "The Depopulation of the Dhegiha-Siouan Kansas Prior to Removal," *New Mexico Historical Review* 48, no. 2 (October 1973): 316–317; Kate L. Gregg, "The History of Fort Osage," *Missouri Historical Review* 34 (October 1939–July 1940): 445.

3 Morse, *Report to the Secretary of War,* 366.

4 George C. Sibley to Governor [William] Clark, February 3, 1819, Clarence E. Carter, comp. and ed., *The Territorial Papers of the United States* (Washington, DC: Government Printing Office, 1934–1962), 15: 516.

5 A Map Exhibiting the Territorial limits of Several Nations & Tribes of Indians agreeable to the notes of A. Chouteau reduced, & laid down on a scale of 80 miles to the inch, by R. Paul, February 1816, Map 884, Tube 702, Record Group 75, Cartographic Branch, National Archives and Records Administration.

6 William E. Foley and C. David Rice, *The First Chouteaus: River Barons of Early St. Louis* (Urbana: University of Illinois Press, 1983), 105, 188, 198.

7 A Map Exhibiting the Territorial limits of Several Nations & Tribes of Indians.

8 Louise Barry, comp., *The Beginning of the West: Annals of the Kansas Gate-*

way to the American West, 1540–1854 (Topeka: Kansas State Historical Society, 1972), 142, 145–146.

9 For a summary of military escorts on the Santa Fe Trail, see Leo E. Oliva, *Soldiers on the Santa Fe Trail* (Norman: University of Oklahoma Press, 1967), 25–54.

10 Barry, *The Beginning of the West*, 163–165.

11 *Niles' Weekly Register*, November 14, 1818.

12 Barry, *The Beginning of the West*, 157.

13 Ibid., 201; William H. Goetzmann, *Exploration and Empire: The Explorer and the Scientist in the Winning of the American West* (New York: Alfred A. Knopf, 1966), 146–149. The best summary of Bonneville's travels and observations is in Washington Irving, *The Adventures of Captain Bonneville, U.S.A., in the Rocky Mountains and Far West, Digested from his Journal by Washington Irving*, ed. Edgeley W. Todd (Norman: University of Oklahoma Press, 1961).

14 John Bidwell, *Journey to California* (San Francisco: J. H. Nash, 1937).

15 Barry, *The Beginning of the West*, 208.

16 Alfred W. Crosby, Jr., "Virgin Soil Epidemics as a Factor in the Aboriginal Depopulation in America," *William and Mary Quarterly* 33 (April 1976): 289. See also Russell Thornton, *American Indian Holocaust and Survival: A Population History since 1492* (Norman: University of Oklahoma Press, 1987), 46–47.

17 *U.S. Statutes at Large* 3 (1932): 514–515. For fur trader opposition and bureaucratic snarl in the government's vaccination program in the St. Louis Superintendency, particularly among the Kansa tribe, see William E. Unrau, "Fur Trader and Indian Office Obstruction to Smallpox Vaccination in the St. Louis Indian Superintendency, 1831–1834," *Plains Anthropologist* 34 (May 1989): 33–39.

18 Report of William Clark, October 20, 1827, Letters Received by the Office of Indian Affairs, Record Group 75, Microfilm 234, St. Louis Superintendency, Roll 748, National Archives and Records Service; William Clark to John Dougherty, October 24, 1827, John Dougherty Papers, Manuscript Division, Missouri Historical Society.

19 Barry, *The Beginning of the West*, 208; David J. Wishart, *An Unspeakable Sadness: The Dispossession of the Nebraska Indians* (Lincoln: University of Nebraska Press, 1994), 63.

20 Isaac McCoy, *History of Baptist Indian Missions: Embracing Remarks on the Former and Present Condition of the Aboriginal Tribes: Their Former Settlement within the Indian Territory, and Their Future Prospects* (Washington, DC: Wm. M. Morrison, 1840), 442–443.

21 Charles J. Kappler, comp., *Indian Affairs: Laws and Treaties* (Washington, DC: Government Printing Office, 1904), 2:416–418; Wishart, *An Unspeakable Sadness*, 61–63.

22 John D. Unruh, Jr., *The Plains Across: The Overland Emigrants and the Trans-Mississippi West, 1840–1860* (Urbana: University of Illinois Press, 1979), 127–129.

23 Larry C. Skogen, *Indian Depredation Claims, 1796–1920* (Norman: University of Oklahoma Press, 1996), 43.

24 Ibid.

25 Unruh, *The Plains Across*, 139–140.

26 Skogen, *Indian Depredation Claims*, 209.

27 Isaac McCoy to Secretary of War John H. Eaton, April n.d., 1831, Correspondence on the Subject on the Emigration of Indians between the 30th of November and 27th of December, 1833, with Abstracts of Expenditures by Disbursing Agents in the Removal and Subsistence of Indians, &c., &c., II, *Senate Executive Document* no. 512, 23-1, serial 245, 436.

28 Report of the Secretary of War, in compliance with a resolution of the Senate, transmitting a report of the expedition of the dragoons, under the command of Colonel Henry Dodge, to the Rocky Mountains, during the summer of 1835, &c., *House Document* no. 181, 24-1, serial 289, 2–3.

29 Matthew C. Field, *Prairie and Mountain Sketches*, coll. Clyde and Mae Reed Porter, ed. Kate L. Gregg and John Francis McDermott (Norman: University of Oklahoma Press, 1957), xxi, xxvi, 34–36.

30 Ibid., 34.

31 Kappler, *Treaties*, 2: 223.

32 See Chapter 3.

33 State of Kansas, compiled chiefly from the official Records of the General Land Office . . . under the direction of L. P. Berthrong, Chief of the Drafting Division, General Land Office, 1925, Map 11321, Tube 1387, Record Group 75, Cartographic Branch, National Archives and Records Service.

34 See Chapter 3, note 55.

35 Kappler, *Treaties*, 2: 304–305; William E. Unrau, *Mixed-Bloods and Tribal Dissolution: Charles Curtis and the Quest for Indian Identity* (Lawrence: University Press of Kansas, 1989), 33.

36 Kappler, *Treaties*, 2: 536.

37 Paul W. Gates, "Indian Allotments Preceding the Dawes Act," in John G. Clark, ed., *The Frontier Challenge: Responses to the Trans-Mississippi West* (Lawrence: University Press of Kansas, 1971), 148, 152–153, 157; Homer E. Socolofsky, "Wyandot Floats," *Kansas Historical Quarterly* 36 (Autumn 1970): 244, 247, 251.

38 Unrau, *Mixed-Bloods and Tribal Dissolution*, 53–61; Socolofsky, "Wyandot Floats," 251–304.

39 L. F. Linn to Hon. Lewis Cass, May 14, 1835, Documents relating to the

extension of the northern boundary line of the State of Missouri, *Senate Document* no. 206, 24-1, serial 281, 6.

40 Howard I. McKee, "The Platte Purchase," *Missouri Historical Review* 32 (January 1938): 132.

41 Pierre Menard and Jno. L. Bean to The Hon. L. F. Linn, February 6, 1835, Documents relating to the extension of the northern boundary line of the State of Missouri, *Senate Document* no. 206, 24-1, serial 281, 2–3.

42 Linn to Cass, May 14, 1835, ibid., 5–6.

43 Skogen, *Indian Depredation Claims*, 43. McKenney's view of Cass is similar to a twentieth-century study that characterizes the secretary of war as "one of the master architects of American Indian policy" and a dedicated public servant who "made every effort to know the land [i.e., Indian country] which was his domain and the people [i.e., the Indians] whom he governed." See Francis Paul Prucha, *Lewis Cass and American Indian Policy* (Detroit: Wayne State University Press, 1967), 1, 17.

44 Cass to Linn, August 27, 1835, Documents relating to the northern boundary line of the State of Missouri, *Senate Document* no. 206, 24-1, serial 181, 8.

45 Extracts from Minutes of a Council held at Prairie du Chien, July, 1830, sent to Secretary War John H. Eaton, William Clark to John H. Eaton, November 19, 1830, Ratified Treaties, 1827–1832, Record Group 75, Target 494, Roll 2, National Archives and Records Administration.

46 Kappler, *Treaties*, 2: 402–403.

47 McKee, "The Platte Purchase," 135–144; *U.S. Statutes at Large* 5 (1837): 802.

48 R. David Edmonds, "Potawatomis in the Platte Country: An Indian Removal Incomplete," *Missouri Historical Review* 68 (July 1974), 386–387.

Chapter Six. Proscription

1 See Chapter 1.

2 Charles J. Kappler, comp., *Indian Affairs: Laws and Treaties* (Washington, DC: Government Printing Office, 1904), 2: 418–588 passim.

3 *U.S. Statutes at Large* 4 (1834): 729–734.

4 Ibid., 4: 564.

5 Peter C. Mancall, *Deadly Medicine: Indians and Alcohol in Early America* (Ithaca, NY: Cornell University Press, 1995), 103.

6 Ibid., 120.

7 For a general account of Indian prohibition in nineteenth-century America, see William E. Unrau, *White Man's Wicked Water: The Alcohol Trade and*

Prohibition in Indian Country, 1802–1892 (Lawrence: University Press of Kansas, 1996).

8 *U.S. Statutes at Large* 2 (1802): 146.

9 Ibid., 2: 243–244.

10 Richard E. Oglesby, *Manuel Lisa and the Opening of the Missouri Fur Trade* (Norman: University of Oklahoma Press, 1963), 173–175.

11 *U.S. Statutes at Large* 3 (1822): 682–683.

12 Colonel J. Snelling to Secretary of War, August 23, 1825, *American State Papers, 2, Indian Affairs,* 2: 661.

13 Kappler, *Treaties,* 2: 93.

14 See Chapter 4.

15 Francis Paul Prucha, *The Great Father: The United States Government and the American Indians* (Lincoln: University of Nebraska Press, 1984), 1: 205.

16 Kickapoo Statement to E. A. Ellsworth, September (?), 1833, Letters Received by the Office of Indian Affairs, Record Group 75, Microfilm 234, Western Superintendency, Roll 921, National Archives and Records Administration.

17 E. A. Ellsworth Talk with Kickapoos, ibid.

18 George Bird Grinnell, "Bent's Old Fort and Its Builders," *Collections of the Kansas State Historical Society* 15 (1919–1922), 45, 58–59.

19 Cited in Grant Foreman, *Advancing the Frontier, 1830–1860* (Norman: University of Oklahoma Press, 1830), 25–26.

20 Lewis Cass, "Remarks on the Policy and Practices of the United States and Great Britain in Their Treatment of the Indians," *North American Review* 24 (April 1827): 404.

21 *U.S. Statutes at Large* 4 (1834): 732.

22 Private Council with the Delaware and Shawnee Chiefs, n.d., 1834, Letters Received by the Office of Indian Affairs, Record Group 75, Microfilm 234, Western Superintendency, Roll 929, National Archives and Records Administration.

23 Ibid.

24 Ibid.

25 Richard M. Cummins to Thomas H. Harvey, January 20, 1848, Letters Received by the Office of Indian Affairs, Record Group 75, Microfilm 234, Fort Leavenworth Agency, Roll 302, National Archives and Records Administration.

26 *History of Clay and Platte Counties* (St. Louis: National Historical, 1885), III, 119, 596; Unrau, *White Man's Wicked Water,* 44.

27 Prucha, *The Great Father,* 1: 171.

28 Unrau, *White Man's Wicked Water,* 45–46; Kappler, *Treaties,* 2: 339–565 passim.

29 Charles P. Deatherage, *Early History of Greater Kansas City Missouri and Kansas* (Kansas City: Charles P. Deatherage, 1927), 1: 334. Another study concludes that the actual *yearly* payment to the removal tribes west of Missouri alone was just over $1,000,000. See William E. Miller, *History of Jackson County* (Kansas City: Birdsall and Williams, 1881), 70.

30 Joseph M. Street to ?, n.d., *Annual Report of the Commissioner of Indian Affairs* (1838), NCR Reprint 872, Roll 4158, 492–493.

31 *U.S. Statutes at Large* 9 (1847): 203.

32 Robert A. Trennert, Jr., *Alternative to Extinction: Federal Indian Policy and the Beginnings of the Reservation System, 1846–51* (Philadelphia: Temple University Press, 1975), 37–38.

33 Orlando Brown to Thomas Ewing, November 30, 1849, *Annual Report of the Commissioner of Indian Affairs* (1849), NCR Reprint 872, Roll 4158, 5.

34 John Dougherty to William Clark, November 10, 1831, Letters Received by the Office of Indian Affairs, Record Group 75, Microfilm 234, St. Louis Superintendency, Roll 749, National Archives and Records Service; Montfort Stokes, Henry L. Ellsworth, and J.T. Schermerhorn to Lewis Cass, February 10, 1834, *Annual Report of the Commissioner of Indian Affairs* (1834), NCR Reprint 872, Roll 4158, 97.

35 Unrau, *White Man's Wicked Water*, 58–62.

36 Alfred J. Vaughan to Thomas H. Harvey, September 20, 1845, *Annual Report of the Commissioner of Indian Affairs* (1845), NCR Reprint 872, Roll 4158, 557.

37 Trennert, *Alternative to Extinction*, 38.

38 Unrau, *White Man's Wicked Water*, 87–88.

39 George F. Ruxton, *Life in the Far West* (Edinburgh: William Blackwood, 1868), 28.

40 William Gay to A. Cumming, May 3, 1856, Letters Received by the Office of Indian Affairs, Record Group 75, Microfilm 234, Shawnee Agency, Roll 809, National Archives and Records Administration.

41 *U.S. Statutes at Large* 9 (1847): 194.

42 Sondra Van Meter McCoy, "Central Kansas Trading Ranches on the Santa Fe Trail," in Leo E. Oliva, ed., *Adventure on the Santa Fe Trail* (Topeka: Kansas State Historical Society, 1988), 110–113.

43 Wm. P. Richardson to D. D. Mitchell, October 21, 1850, A. M. Upshaw to John Drennon, August 29, 1849, Thomas Mosely, Jr. to D. D. Mitchell, August 25, 1851, George W. Manypenny to R. McClelland, November 26, 1853, *Annual Report(s) of the Commissioner of Indian Affairs* (1849, 1850, 1851, and 1853), NCR Reprint 872, Roll 4158, 30–31 (1849), 190 (1850), 79 (1851), and 22 (1853).

44 *U.S. Statutes at Large* 12 (1862): 339.

45 Section 2139, *Revised Statutes of the United States Passed at the First Session*

of the Forty-Third Congress, 1872–1873 (Washington, DC: Government Printing Office, 1875), 375.

46 *Bates v. Clark,* 95 U.S. 204 (1877).

47 Felix S. Cohen, *Handbook of Federal Indian Law* (Washington, DC: Government Printing Office, 1942), 7.

48 See Chapter 1.

49 *Bates v. Clark,* 207.

50 Robert A. Trennert, Jr., "The Mormons and the Office of Indian Affairs: The Conflict over Winter Quarters, 1846–1848," *Nebraska History* 53, no. 3 (Fall 1972): 384–396; Richard E. Bennett, *Mormons at the Missouri, 1846–1852: "and Should We Die—"* (Norman: University of Oklahoma Press, 1987), 94, 101–110; David J. Wishart, *An Unspeakable Sadness: The Dispossession of the Nebraska Indians* (Lincoln: University of Nebraska Press, 1994), 87. See also Judith A. Boughter, *Betraying the Omaha Nation, 1790–1916* (Norman: University of Oklahoma Press, 1998), 49–52.

51 See Chapter 2.

52 Ibid.

53 Edwin Bryant, *What I Saw in California* (1848; repr. with an introduction by Thomas D. Clark, Lincoln: University of Nebraska Press, 1985), 56.

Chapter Seven. Compression

1 George A. Schultz, *An Indian Canaan: Isaac McCoy and the Vision of an Indian State* (Norman: University of Oklahoma Press, 1972), 194.

2 Ronald N. Satz, *American Indian Policy in the Jacksonian Era* (Lincoln: University of Nebraska Press, 1975), 142–143.

3 John D. Unruh, Jr., *The Plains Across: The Overland Emigrants and the Trans-Mississippi West, 1840–1860* (Urbana: University of Illinois Press, 1979), 117–121; John Mack Farragher, *Women and Men on the Overland Trail* (New Haven, CT: Yale University Press, 1979), 31–32.

4 Robert A. Trennert, Jr., *Alternative to Extinction: Federal Indian Policy and the Beginnings of the Reservation System, 1846–51* (Philadelphia: Temple University Press, 1979), 29–31; James C. Malin, "Indian Policy and Westward Expansion," *Bulletin of the University of Kansas Humanistic Studies,* 2 (1921): 77–78.

5 Lewis Cass to Genl. Wm. Marshall, July 12, 1834, Documents Relating to the Negotiation of the Treaty of October 23, 1834, with the Miami Indians, Documents Relating to the Negotiation of Ratified and Unratified Treaties, Ratified Treaties, 1832–1838, Record Group 75, Target 494, Roll 3, National

Archives and Records Administration. The map referenced by Cass was not found in the Miami Treaty file for 1834.

6 Charles J. Kappler, comp., *Indian Affairs: Laws and Treaties* (Washington, DC: Government Printing Office, 1904), 2: 426–428.

7 Malin, "Indian Policy and Westward Expansion," 80–83.

8 Trennert, *Alternative to Extinction,* 29, 195.

9 State of Kansas, compiled chiefly from Official Records of the General Land Office with supplemental data from other map making agencies, under the direction of L.P. Berthrong, Chief of the Drafting Division, G.L.O., 1925, Map 11321, Tube 1387, Kansas or Kaw Indians vs. United States (Court of Claims F-64), June 1, 1932, Records of the Bureau of Indian Affairs, Cartographic Branch, Record Group 75, National Archives and Records Administration.

10 William Clark to James Barbour, November 30, 1825, Documents Relating to the Negotiation of Ratified and Unratified Treaties with the Various Tribes of Indians, 1801–69, Introduction and Ratified Treaties, 1801–26, Record Group 75, Target 494, Roll 1, National Archives and Records Administration.

11 Robert Joseph Keckeisen, "The Kansa 'Half-Breed' Lands: Contravention and Transformation of United States Indian Policy in Kansas" (M.A. thesis, Wichita State University, 1977), 33–34.

12 Kappler, *Treaties,* 2: 224.

13 Thomas Harvey to William Medill, December 12, 1848, Letters Received by the Office of Indian Affairs, Record Group 75, Microfilm 234, Fort Leavenworth Agency, Roll 302, National Archives and Records Administration; John S. Phillips to Medill, February 7, 1849, Letters Received by the Office of Indian Affairs, Record Group 75, Microfilm 234, St. Louis Superintendency, Roll 755, National Archives and Records Administration.

14 Kappler, *Treaties,* 2: 526.

15 Ibid., 2: 552–554.

16 William E. Unrau, *The Kansa Indians: A History of the Wind People, 1673–1873* (Norman: University of Oklahoma Press, 1971), 161–163, 166.

17 Malin, "Indian Policy and Westward Expansion," 102, map 3.

18 Kappler, *Treaties,* 2: 553.

19 Harvey to Richard W. Cummins, May 15, 1847, Letters Received by the Office of Indian Affairs, Record Group 75, Microfilm 234, Roll 302, Fort Leavenworth Agency, National Archives and Records Administration; Unrau, *The Kansa Indians,* 162.

20 Louise Barry, comp., *The Beginning of the West: Annals of the Kansas Gateway to the American West, 1540–1854* (Topeka: Kansas State Historical Society,

1972), 784; Charles Preuss, *Exploring with Fremont: The Private Diaries of Charles Preuss, Cartographer for John C. Fremont on His First, Second, and Fourth Expeditions to the Far West,* trans. and ed. Erwin G. and Elisabeth K. Gudde (Norman: University of Oklahoma Press, 1958), 143.

21 Barry, *The Beginning of the West,* 949–950; Morris F. Taylor, *First Mail West: Stagecoach Lines on the Santa Fe Trail* (Albuquerque: University of New Mexico Press, 1972), 8.

22 George W. Clarke to Alfred Cumming, November 7, 1854, Letters Received by the Office of Indian Affairs, Record Group 75, Microfilm 234, Potawatomi Agency, Roll 679, National Archives and Records Administration.

23 On November 28, 1856, Kansa Indian Agent John Montgomery reported that the 1854 Seth Eastman survey of the Kansa lands as established by the 1846 treaty was incorrect, and that the Council Grove town site was on Kansa reservation land. See William E. Unrau, "The Council Grove Merchants and Kansa Indians, 1855–1870," *Kansas Historical Quarterly* 24, no. 3 (Autumn 1968): 272.

Chapter Eight. Intrusion

1 Stephen A. Douglas to J. H. Crane, D. M. Johnson, and L. J. Eastin, December 17, 1853, *The Letters of Stephen A. Douglas,* ed. Robert W. Johannsen (Urbana: University of Illinois Press, 1969), 269–270; James C. Malin, "The Motives of Stephen A. Douglas in the Organization of Nebraska Territory: A Letter Dated December 17, 1853," *Kansas Historical Quarterly* 19 (November 1951): 321–353; Francis Paul Prucha, *The Great Father: The United States Government and the American Indians* (Lincoln: University of Nebraska Press, 1984), 1: 346.

2 Quish-Queh-Leh, his + mark, to President of the United States, November 20, 1835, Report from Committee on Indian Affairs, on the Resolution Relative to Exchanging Lands with the Pottawatomie Indians, &c., *Senate Document* no. 348, 24-1, serial 283, 348.

3 *Congressional Globe,* February 17, 1854, 33-1, *Appendix,* 23, p. 153.

4 Ibid., May 9, 1854, 6362.

5 Edward Everett Hale, *Kansas and Nebraska: The History, Geographical and Physical Characteristics and Political Position of these Territories: An Account of the Emigrant Aid Companies, and Directions to Emigrants* (Boston: Phillips, Sampson, 1854), 216–217.

6 Rev. C. G. Boynton and T. B. Mason, *A Journey through Kansas; with Sketches of Nebraska: Describing the Country, Climate, Soil, Minerals, Manufacturing, and Other Resources. The Results of a Tour in the Autumn of 1854* (Cincinnati: Moore, Wilstach, Keys, 1855), 152–154.

7 Ibid., 118–119.

8 *National Intelligencer* (Washington, DC), November 5, 1853.

9 *U.S. Statutes at Large* 10 (1853): 238.

10 Robert M. Kvasnicka, "George W. Manypenny," in Robert M. Kvasnicka and Herman J. Viola, eds., *The Commissioners of Indian Affairs, 1824–1977* (Lincoln: University of Nebraska Press, 1979), 57–58. According to Paul Wallace Gates, when the Kansas-Nebraska Territory became a legal reality (May 30, 1854), "there was not within it an acre of land that was available for sale." Paul Wallace Gates, *Fifty Million Acres: Conflicts over Kansas Land Policy, 1854–1890* (Ithaca, NY: Cornell University Press, 1954), 3.

11 *National Intelligencer* (Washington, DC), November 5, 1853.

12 George W. Manypenny to Robert McClelland, November 9, 1853, Letters Received by the Indian Division, 1849–80, Records of the Office of the Secretary of the Interior, Record Group 48, Box 2, National Archives and Records Administration.

13 Manypenny to McClelland, November 9, 1853, Letters Received by the Indian Division, 1849–80, Records of the Office of the Secretary of the Interior, Record Group 48, Box 2, National Archives and Records Administration. See also George W. Manypenny, *Our Indian Wards* (1880, repr., New York: Da Capo Press, 1972), 117–122.

14 Isaac McCoy to Secretary of War John H. Eaton, September 30, 1830, and April n.d., 1832, Correspondence on the Subject of the Emigration of Indians between the 30th of November and 27th of December, 1833, with Abstracts of Expenditures by Disbursing Agents in the Removal and Subsistence of Indians, &c., &c., 2, *Senate Executive Document*, no. 512, 23-1, serial 245, 436.

15 *Congressional Globe*, January 29, 1851, 31-2, *Appendix*, 137, quoted in Henry Nash Smith, *Virgin Land: The American West as Symbol and Myth* (Cambridge, MA: Harvard University Press, 1950, 1978), 171.

16 Smith, *Virgin Land*, 22.

17 Joint Committee on Printing, Congress of the United States, comp. and ed., *Biographical Directory of the United States Congress, 1774–1989* (Washington, DC: Government Printing Office, 1989), 612.

18 Manypenny, *Our Indian Wards*, 117.

19 Louise Barry, comp., *The Beginning of the West: Annals of the Kansas Gateway to the American West, 1540–1854* (Topeka: Kansas State Historical Society, 1972), 1178.

20 George W. Manypenny to Sen. David R. Atchison, August 10, 1853. Letters Received by the Indian Division, 1849–80, Records of the Office of the Secretary of the Interior, Record Group 48, Box 2, National Archives and Records Administration.

21 Charles J. Kappler, comp., *Indian Affairs: Laws and Treaties* (Washington, DC: Government Printing Office, 1904), 2: 594–595.

22 H. Craig Miner and William E. Unrau, *The End of Indian Kansas: A Study of Cultural Revolution, 1854–1871* (Lawrence: Regents Press of Kansas, 1978), 7–8; William E. Unrau, *White Man's Wicked Water: The Alcohol Trade and Prohibition in Indian Country, 1802–1892* (Lawrence: University Press of Kansas, 1996), 82; Barry, *The Beginning of the West*, 1146, 1202.

23 James C. Malin, *The Nebraska Question, 1852–1854* (Lawrence, KS: Author, 1953), 128–136, 152; *Missouri Democrat* (St. Louis), June 30, August 13, October 18, 1853; *Liberty Weekly Tribune* (Liberty, MO), September 16, 1853; *Gazette* (St. Joseph, MO), June 8, 22, 23, 1853; *National Intelligencer* (Washington, DC), November 5, 1853.

24 *Missouri Democrat* (St. Louis), April 17, 1853; Miner and Unrau, *The End of Indian Kansas*, 10–11.

25 *U.S. Statutes at Large* 10 (1854): 310; Gates, *Fifty Million Acres*, 21.

26 Acting Secretary of the Interior George C. Whiting to President of the United States, October 21, 1854, Records of the Office of the Secretary of the Interior, Record Group 48, Microfilm 606, Special Classes of Letters Sent, Indian Division, Interior Department, Roll 2, National Archives and Records Administration.

27 Benjamin F. Robinson to Alfred Cumming, October 30, 1854, Letter from the Secretary of the Interior Transmitting Reports in Reference to Carrying Out of the Treaty Stipulations with the Delaware Indians, February 3, 1855, *House Executive Document* no. 50, 33-2, serial 783, p. 38.

28 Barry, *The Beginning of the West*, 1202.

29 John Montgomery to Alfred Cumming, October 5, 1855, Letters Received by the Office of Indian Affairs, Record Group 75, Microfilm 234, Kansas Agency, Roll 364, National Archives and Records Service.

30 George Clarke to Alfred Cumming, March 29, 1856, Letters Received by the Office of Indian Affairs, Record Group 75, Microfilm 234, Potawatomi Agency, Roll 680, National Archives and Records Service. For an especially unfortunate example of missionary success in securing title to Indian country land, see Article 2 of the Kansa Treaty of March 13, 1862, whereby Thomas Sears Huffaker was given 640 acres of prime Kansa reservation land at Council Grove "on which he has resided and improved and cultivated since the year A.D. 1851," Kappler, *Treaties*, 2: 829.

31 In *Ex Parte Crow Dog*, 109 U.S. 556 (1883), it was determined that reservation land within a territory in which Indian title had not been extinguished remained Indian country as defined by the Indian Trade and Intercourse Act of

1834. See also Felix S. Cohen, *Handbook of Federal Indian Law* (Washington, DC: Government Printing Office, 1942), 7.

32 *Missouri Republican* (St. Louis), July 1, 1854, quoted in Barry, *The Beginning of the West,* 1231.

33 *Daily Tribune* (New York), July 13, 1854, quoted in Barry, *The Beginning of the West,* 1231.

34 *Missouri Republican* (St. Louis), July 12, 1854, quoted in Barry, *The Beginning of the West,* 1232.

35 Miner and Unrau, *The End of Indian Kansas,* 21–23; "Governor Reeder's Administration," *Transactions of the Kansas State Historical Society* 5 (1896): 166–169.

Chapter Nine. Illusion

1 James H. Shortridge, *Peopling the Plains: Who Settled Where in Frontier Kansas* (Lawrence: University Press of Kansas, 1995), 1.

2 Those Indians who "endured" were bands or splinter groups of Kickapoo, Potawatomi, Chippewa, Munsee, Iowa, and Sac people. See Joseph B. Herring, *The Enduring Indians of Kansas: A Century and a Half of Acculturation* (Lawrence: University Press of Kansas, 1990), 1. For the removal of Indians from Kansas to present-day Oklahoma after 1854, see H. Craig Miner and William E. Unrau, *The End of Indian Kansas: A Study of Cultural Revolution, 1854–1871* (Lawrence: Regents Press of Kansas, 1978). In terms of human suffering the removal was made worse by the irruption of a major smallpox epidemic in the spring of 1855, which resulted in 400 fatalities among the Kansa Indians alone: John Montgomery to Alexander Cumming, August 31, 1855, Letters Received by the Office of Indian Affairs, Record Group 75, Microfilm 234, Kansas Agency, Roll 364, National Archives and Records Administration.

3 John C. McCoy to George W. Manypenny, October 10, 1855, Letters Received by the Office of Indian Affairs, Record Group 75, Microfilm 234, Shawnee Agency, Roll 809, National Archives and Records Service.

4 Paul Wallace Gates, *Fifty Million Acres: Conflicts over Kansas Land Policy, 1854–1890* (Ithaca, NY: Cornell University Press, 1954), 3.

5 Miner and Unrau, *The End of Indian Kansas,* 116.

6 *National Intelligencer* (Washington, DC), May 24, 1855.

7 Robert M. Kvasnicka, "George W. Manypenny," in Robert M. Kvasnicka and Herman J. Viola, eds., *The Commissioners of Indian Affairs, 1824–1977* (Lincoln: University of Nebraska Press, 1979), 58–60; Francis Paul Prucha, *The Great*

Father: The United States Government and the American Indians (Lincoln: University of Nebraska Press, 1984), 1: 347.

8 George W. Manypenny, *Our Indian Wards* (New York: Da Capo Press, 1972, reprint of the original published by Robert Clark, Cincinnati, 1880), 122–123.

9 See Chapters 3 and 8.

10 Charles J. Kappler, comp., *Indian Affairs: Laws and Treaties* (Washington, DC: Government Printing Office, 1904), 2: 262–264, 335–336.

11 See Chapter 3.

12 Kappler, *Treaties*, 2: 247, 249.

13 Manypenny, *Our Indian Wards*, 111.

14 Ibid., 122–123.

15 Charles Mix to J. Thompson, December 9, 1857, General Incoming Correspondence, Indian Division, Interior Department, 1854–1857, Records of the Office of Secretary of the Interior, Record Group 48, Box 6, National Archives and Records Administration.

16 See Chapter 8.

17 *United States v. Downing,* Fed. Cas. No. 14-903 (Kan. 1876), *Central Law Journal,* 383.

18 Alexander Ramsey to Luke Lea, October 21, 1850, cited in William E. Unrau, *White Man's Wicked Water: The Alcohol Trade and Prohibition in Indian Country, 1802–1892* (Lawrence: University Press of Kansas, 1996), 77.

19 *Bates v. Clark,* 95 U.S. 204 (1877).

20 Terry P. Wilson, *The Underground Reservation: Osage Oil* (Lincoln: University of Nebraska Press, 1985), passim.

21 18 *United States Code* 1151. The exceptions are in Sections 1154 and 1156.

Sources

Unpublished Government Records

A Map Exhibiting the Territorial Limits of Several Nations and Tribes of Indians Agreeable to the notes of A. Chouteau reduced, & laid down on a scale of 80 miles to the inch, by R. Paul, February 1816. Map 884, Tube 702, Record Group 75, Cartographic Branch, National Archives and Records Administration.

Documents Relating to the Negotiation of Ratified and Unratified Treaties with the Various Tribes of Indians, 1801–69, Introduction and Ratified Treaties, 1801–1826, Record Group 75, Target 494, Rolls 1–4, National Archives and Records Administration.

General Incoming Correspondence, Indian Division, Interior Department, 1854–1857, Records of the Office of the Secretary of the Interior, Record Group 48, Box 6, National Archives and Records Administration.

Letters Received by the Indian Division, 1848–80, Records of the Office of the Secretary of the Interior, Record Group 48, Box 2, National Archives and Records Administration.

Letters Received by the Office of Indian Affairs, Record Group 75, Microfilm 234, Fort Leavenworth Agency, Roll 302, National Archives and Records Administration.

Letters Received by the Office of Indian Affairs, Record Group 75, Microfilm 234, Kansas Agency, Roll 364, 365, National Archives and Records Administration.

Letters Received by the Office of Indian Affairs, Record Group 75, Microfilm 234, Kiowa-Comanche Agency, Roll 375, National Archives and Records Administration.

Letters Received by the Office of Indian Affairs, Record Group 75, Microfilm 234, Osage Agency, Roll 631, National Archives and Records Administration.

Letters Received by the Office of Indian Affairs, Record Group 75, Microfilm 234, Miami Agency, Roll 416, National Archives and Records Administration.

Letters Received by the Office of Indian Affairs, Record Group 75, Microfilm 234, Potawatomi Agency, Roll 679, 680, National Archives and Records Administration.

Letters Received by the Office of Indian Affairs, Record Group 75, Microfilm 234, Shawnee Agency, Roll 809, National Archives and Records Administration.

Letters Received by the Office of Indian Affairs, Record Group 75, Microfilm 234, St. Louis Superintendency, Rolls 748–749, 755, National Archives and Records Administration.

Letters Received by the Office of Indian Affairs, Record Group 75, Microfilm 234, Western Superintendency, Roll 921, National Archives and Records Administration.

Records of the Office of the Secretary of the Interior, Record Group 48, Microfilm 606, Special Classes of Letters Sent, Indian Division, Interior Department, Roll 2, National Archives and Records Administration.

Records of the Office of the Secretary of the Interior, Record Group 107, Microfilm 6, Letters Sent, Military Affairs, 1800–1861, Rolls 13, 14, National Archives and Records Service.

State of Kansas, compiled chiefly from the official Records of the General Land Office . . . under the direction of L. P. Berthrong, Chief of the Drafting Division, General Land Office, 1925, Map 11321, Tube 1387, Record Group 75, Cartographic Branch, National Archives and Records Administration.

Published Government Records

American State Papers: 2, Indian Affairs. 2 vols. Gales and Seaton, 1832–1834.

Annual Reports of the Commissioner of Indian Affairs (1834–1853). NCR Reprint 872, Roll 4158.

Carter, Clarence E., comp. and ed. *The Territorial Papers of the United States.* 26 vols. Washington: Government Printing Office, 1934–1962.

Congressional Globe, 31-2, 33-1.

House Executive Document no. 2, 20-2, serial 175.

House Executive Document no. 50, 33-2, serial 783.

House Document no. 1, 19-1, serial 131.

House Document no. 117, 19-1, serial 136.

House Document no. 172, 22-1, serial 219.

House Document no. 181, 24-1, serial 289.

House Report no. 474, 23-1, serial 263.

Kappler, Charles J., comp. *Indian Affairs: Law and Treaties*. 5 vols. Washington: United States Government Printing Office, 1904.

Register of Debates in Congress.

Revised Statutes of the United States Passed at the First Session of the Forty-Third Congress, 1872–1873. Washington: Government Printing Office, 1875.

Royce, Charles C. *Indian Land Cessions in the United States*. Eighteenth Annual Report of the Bureau of American Ethnology, 1896–1897, part 2. Washington: Government Printing Office, 1899.

Senate Document no. 72, 20-2, serial 181.

Senate Document no. 206, 24-1, serial 281.

Senate Document no. 348, 24-1, serial 283.

Senate Executive Document no. 512, 23-1, serial 245.

United States Code.

United States Statutes at Large.

Manuscript Collections

John Dougherty Papers, Manuscript Division, Missouri Historical Society.

George C. Sibley Papers, Manuscript Division, Missouri Historical Society.

Second Colorado Regiment Veterans Papers, Manuscript Division, State Historical Society of Colorado.

Newspapers

Gazette (St. Joseph, MO).

Liberty Weekly Tribune (Liberty, MO).

Missouri Democrat (St. Louis).

National Intelligencer (Washington, DC).

Niles' Weekly Register (Baltimore).

Rocky Mountain News (Denver).

Court Cases

Bates v. Clark, 95 U.S. 204 (1877).

Ex Parte Crow Dog, 109 U. S. 556 (1883).

Johnson and Graham's Lessee v. McIntosh, 8 Wheaton 592 (1823).

United States v. Downing, Fed. Cas. No. 14-903 (Kan. 1876), *Central Law Journal,* 383.

Books

Barry, Louise, comp. *The Beginning of the West: Annals of the Kansas Gateway to the American West, 1540–1854.* Topeka: Kansas State Historical Society, 1972.

Bennett, Richard E. *Mormons at the Missouri, 1846–1852: "and Should We Die—."* Norman: University of Oklahoma Press, 1987.

Bidwell, John. *Journey to California.* San Francisco: J. H. Nash, 1937.

Boughter, Judith A. *Betraying the Omaha Nation, 1790–1916.* Norman: University of Oklahoma Press, 1998.

Boynton, Rev. C. G., and T. B. Mason, *A Journey through Kansas; with Sketches of Nebraska: Describing the Country, Climate, Soil, Minerals, Manufacturing, and Other Resources. The Results of a Tour in the Autumn of 1854.* Cincinnati: Moore, Wilstach, Keys, 1855.

Brackenridge, Henry Marie. *Views of Louisiana Together with a Journal of a Voyage up the Missouri River, in 1811.* Pittsburgh: Cramer, Spear and Eichbaum, 1814. Reprint, Chicago: Quadrangle Books, 1962.

Bradbury, John. *Travels in the Interior of America in the Years 1809, 1810, and 1811.* Liverpool: Smith and Galloway, 1817. Reprint, Readex Microprint, 1966.

Bryant, Edwin. *What I Saw in California.* 1848. Reprinted with an introduction by Thomas D. Clark. Lincoln: University of Nebraska Press, 1985.

Caldwell, Martha B., ed. *Annals of the Shawnee Methodist Mission and Indian Manual Labor School.* Topeka: Kansas State Historical Society, 1930.

Cohen, Felix S. *Handbook of Federal Indian Law.* Washington, DC: Government Printing Office, 1942.

Cutler, Jervis. *A Topographical Description of the State of Ohio, Indian Territory, and Louisiana . . . to Which Is Added an Interesting Journal of Mr. Charles Le Raye While Captive with the Sioux Nation on the Waters of the Missouri River.* Boston: Charles Williams–J. Belcher Printer, 1812.

Deatherage, Charles P. *Early History of Greater Kansas City Missouri and Kansas.* Kansas City: Charles P. Deatherage, 1927.

Deloria, Vine, Jr., *Custer Died for Your Sins: An Indian Manifesto.* New York: Macmillan, 1969.

DeVoto, Bernard. *The Year of Decision, 1846.* Cambridge, MA: Riverside Press, 1942.

Ellsworth, Henry Leavitt. *Washington Irving on the Prairie or a Narrative of a Tour of the Southwest in the Year 1832.* Edited by Stanley T. Williams and Barbara D. Simpson. New York: American Book, 1937.

Farragher, John Mack. *Women and Men on the Overland Trail.* New Haven, CT: Yale University Press, 1979.

Field, Matthew C. *Prairie and Mountain Sketches.* Collected by Clyde and Mae Reed Porter and edited by Kate L. Gregg and John Francis McDermott. Norman: University of Oklahoma Press, 1957.

Fixico, Donald L. *The Invasion of Indian Country: American Capitalism and Tribal Natural Resources.* Niwot: University Press of Colorado, 1998.

Foley, William E., and C. David Rice. *The First Chouteaus: River Barons of Early St. Louis.* Urbana: University of Illinois Press, 1983.

Ford, Paul Leicester, ed. *The Works of Thomas Jefferson.* 12 vols. New York: G. P. Putnam's Sons, 1905.

Foreman, Grant. *Advancing the Frontier, 1830–1860.* Norman: University of Oklahoma Press, 1930.

Frazer, Robert W. *Forts of the West: Military Forts and Presidios and Posts Commonly Called Forts West of the Mississippi River to 1898.* Norman: University of Oklahoma Press, 1965.

Gates, Paul Wallace. *Fifty Million Acres: Conflicts over Kansas Land Policy, 1854–1890.* Ithaca, NY: Cornell University Press, 1954.

Goetzmann, William H. *Exploration and Empire: The Explorer and the Scientist in the Winning of the American West.* New York: Alfred A. Knopf, 1966.

Green, Michael E. *The Politics of Indian Removal: Creek Government and Society in Crisis.* Lincoln: University of Nebraska Press, 1982.

Hale, Edward Everett. *Kansas and Nebraska: The History, Geographical and Physical Characteristics and Political Position of these Territories: An Account of the Emigrant Aid Companies, and Directions to Emigrants.* Boston: Phillips, Sampson, 1854.

Herring, Joseph B. *The Enduring Indians of Kansas: A Century and a Half of Acculturation.* Lawrence: University Press of Kansas, 1995.

Hill, Edward H. *The Office of Indian Affairs, 1824–1880: Historical Sketches.* New York: Clearwater Publishing, 1974.

History of Clay and Platte Counties. St. Louis: National Historical Company, 1885.

Hulbert, Archer Butler, ed. *Southwest on the Turquoise Trail: The First Diaries on the Road to Santa Fe.* Colorado Springs: Stewart Commission of Colorado College, 1933; Denver: Denver Public Library, 1933.

Hyde, George E. *A Life of George Bent Written from His Letters.* Edited by Savoie Lottinville. Norman: University of Oklahoma Press, 1967.

Irving, Washington. *The Adventures of Captain Bonneville, U.S.A., in the Rocky Mountains and Far West, Digested from his Journal by Washington Irving.* Edited by Edgeley W. Todd. Norman: University of Oklahoma Press, 1961.

Jackson, Richard H., ed. *The Mormon Role in the Settlement of the West.* Provo, Utah: Brigham Young University Press, 1978.

Joint Committee on Printing, Congress of the United States, comp. and ed. *Biographical Directory of the United States Congress, 1774–1989.* Washington, DC: Government Printing Office, 1989.

Klunder, Willard Carl. *Lewis Cass and the Politics of Moderation.* Kent, OH: Kent State University Press, 1996.

Lawson, Merle Paul. *The Climate of the Great American Desert: Reconstruction of the Climate of Western Interior United States, 1800–1850.* Lincoln: University of Nebraska Press, 1974.

Lienhard, Heinrich. *From St. Louis to Sutter's Fort, 1846.* Translated by Edwin G. and Elisabeth K. Gudde. Norman: University of Oklahoma Press, 1961.

McCoy, Isaac. *History of Baptist Indian Missions: Embracing Remarks on the Former and Present Condition of the Aboriginal Tribes: Their Former Settlement within the Indian Territory, and Their Future Prospects.* Washington: Wm. M. Morrison, 1840.

Malin, James C. *The Grassland of North America, Prolegomena to Its History with Addenda and Postscript.* Gloucester, MA: Peter Smith, 1967.

———. *The Nebraska Question, 1852–1854.* Lawrence, KS: Author, 1953.

Mancall, Peter C. *Deadly Medicine: Indian and Alcohol in Early America.* Ithaca, NY: Cornell University Press, 1995.

Manypenny, George W. *Our Indian Wards.* Cincinnati: Robert Clark & Co., 1880. Reprint, New York: De Capo Press, 1972.

Marshall, Thomas M., ed. *Early Records of Gilpin County, Colorado, 1859–1861.* Denver: W. F. Robinson, 1920.

Mathews, John Joseph. *The Osages: Children of the Middle Waters.* Norman: University of Oklahoma Press, 1961.

Miller, William E. *History of Jackson County.* Kansas City: Birdsall and Williams, 1881.

Miner, H. Craig, and William E. Unrau. *The End of Indian Kansas: A History of Cultural Revolution, 1854–1871.* Lawrence: Regents Press of Kansas, 1978.

Morse, Rev. Jedidiah. *Report to the Secretary of War of the United States on Indian*

Affairs, Comprising a Narrative of a Tour Performed in the Summer of 1820. New Haven, CT: S. Converse, 1822.

Nichols, Roger L. *General Henry Atkinson, A Western Military Career.* Norman: University of Oklahoma Press, 1965.

Oglesby, Richard E. *Manuel Lisa and the Opening of the Missouri Fur Trade.* Norman: University of Oklahoma Press, 1963.

Oliva, Leo E. *Soldiers on the Santa Fe Trail.* Norman: University of Oklahoma Press, 1967.

Phillips, William. *The Conquest of Kansas, by Missouri and Her Allies.* Boston: Phillips, Sampson, and Company, 1856.

Preuss, Charles. *Exploring with Fremont: The Private Diaries of Charles Preuss, Cartographer for John C. Fremont on His First, Second, and Fourth Expeditions to the Far West.* Translated and edited by Erwin G. and Elisabeth K. Gudde. Norman: University of Oklahoma Press, 1958.

Prucha, Francis Paul. *American Indian Policy in the Formative Years: The Indian Trade and Intercourse Acts, 1790–1834.* Cambridge, MA: Harvard University Press, 1962.

———. *The Great Father, The United States Government and the American Indian.* 2 vols. Lincoln: University of Nebraska Press, 1984.

———. *Lewis Cass and American Indian Policy.* Detroit: Wayne State University Press, 1967.

Richardson, James D., comp. *A Compilation of the Messages and Papers of the Presidents, 1789–1897.* 10 vols. Washington, DC: Government Printing Office, 1896–1899.

Rollings, Willard H. *The Osage: An Ethnohistorical Study of Hegemony on the Prairie-Plains.* Columbia: University of Missouri Press, 1992.

Ronda, James P. *Finding the West: Explorations with Lewis and Clark.* Albuquerque: University of New Mexico Press, 2001.

———. *Lewis and Clark among the Indians.* Lincoln: University of Nebraska Press, 1984.

Ruxton, George F. *Life in the Far West.* Edinburgh: William Blackwood, 1868.

Satz, Ronald N. *American Indian Policy in the Jacksonian Era.* Lincoln: University of Nebraska Press, 1975.

Schultz, George A. *An Indian Canaan: Isaac McCoy and the Vision of an Indian State.* Norman: University of Oklahoma Press, 1972.

Sheehan, Bernard. *Seeds of Extinction: Jeffersonian Philanthropy and the American Indian.* New York: W. W. Norton, 1974.

Shortridge, James H. *Peopling the Plains: Who Settled Where in Frontier Kansas.* Lawrence: University Press of Kansas, 1995.

Skogen, Larry C. *Indian Depredation Claims, 1796–1920.* Norman: University of Oklahoma Press, 1996.

Smith, Henry Nash. *Virgin Land: The American West as Symbol and Myth.* Cambridge, MA: Harvard University Press, 1950, 1978.

Steffan, Jerome O. *William Clark: Jeffersonian Man on the Frontier.* Norman: University of Oklahoma Press, 1977.

Taylor, Morris F. *First Mail West: Stagecoach Lines on the Santa Fe Trail.* Albuquerque: University of New Mexico Press, 1972.

The Letters of Stephen A. Douglas. Edited by Robert W. Johannsen. Urbana: University of Illinois Press, 1969.

The Writings of Thomas Jefferson. 20 vols. Washington, DC: Thomas Jefferson Memorial Association, 1905.

Thornton, Russell. *American Indian Holocaust and Survival: A Population History since 1492.* Norman: University of Oklahoma Press, 1987.

Thwaites, Reuben Gold, ed. *Original Journals of the Lewis and Clark Expedition, 1804–1806.* 8 vols. New York: Dodd, Mead, 1904–05.

Trennert, Robert A., Jr. *Alternative to Extinction: Federal Indian Policy and the Beginnings of the Reservation System, 1846–51.* Philadelphia: Temple University Press, 1975.

Unrau, William W. *The Kansa Indians: A History of the Wind People, 1673–1873.* Norman: University of Oklahoma Press, 1971.

———. *Mixed-Bloods and Tribal Dissolution: Charles Curtis and the Quest for Indian Identity.* Lawrence: University Press of Kansas, 1989.

———. *White Man's Wicked Water: The Alcohol Trade and Prohibition in Indian Country, 1802–1892.* Lawrence: University Press of Kansas, 1996.

Unrau, William W., and H. Craig Miner. *Tribal Dispossession and the Ottawa Indian University Fraud.* Norman: University of Oklahoma Press, 1985.

Unruh, John D., Jr. *The Plains Across: The Overland Emigrants and the Trans-Mississippi West, 1840–1860.* Urbana: University of Illinois Press, 1979.

Wishart, David J. *An Unspeakable Sadness: The Dispossession of the Nebraska Indians.* Lincoln: University of Nebraska Press, 1994.

Articles

Abing, Kevin. "Before Bleeding Kansas: Christian Missionaries, Slavery, and the Shawnee Indians in Pre-Territorial Kansas, 1844–1854." *Kansas History: A Journal of the Central Plains* 24, no. 1 (Spring 2001).

Bowden, Martin J. "The Perception of the Western Interior of the United

States, 1800–1870: A Problem in Geosophy." *Proceedings of the Association of American Geographers* 1 (1969).

Brown, Elizabeth Gasser. "Lewis Cass and the American Indian." *Michigan History* 37 (September 1953).

Buford, Rowland, ed. "Report of the Commissioners on the Road from Missouri to New Mexico, October 27 [1825]." *New Mexico Historical Review* 14, no. 3 (July 1939).

Cass, Lewis. "Remarks on the Policy and Practices of the United States and Great Britain in Their Treatment of the Indians." *North American Review* 24 (April 1827).

Crosby, Alfred W., Jr. "Virgin Soil Epidemics as a Factor in the Aboriginal Depopulation in America." *William and Mary Quarterly* 33 (April 1976).

Edmonds, R. David. "Potawatomis in the Platte Country: An Indian Removal Incomplete." *Missouri Historical Review* 68 (July 1974).

Foreman, Carolyn Thomas. "Colonel Jesse Henry Leavenworth." *Chronicles of Oklahoma* 13, no. 1 (March 1933).

Gates, Paul W. "Indian Allotments Preceding the Dawes Act," in John G. Clark, ed., *The Frontier Challenge: Responses to the Trans-Mississippi West.* Lawrence: University Press of Kansas, 1971.

"Governor Reeder's Administration." *Transactions of the Kansas State Historical Society* 5 (1896).

"Great Osage Mission." *Missionary Herald* 19 (July 1823).

Gregg, Kate L. "The History of Fort Osage." *Missouri Historical Review* 34 (October 1939–July 1940).

Grinnell, George Bird. "Bent's Old Fort and Its Builders." *Collections of the Kansas State Historical Society* 15 (1919–1922).

Isern, Thomas D., ed. "Exploration and Diplomacy: George Champlin Sibley's Report to William Clark." *Missouri Historical Review* 73, no. 1 (October 1978).

Klopfenstein, Carl G. "Westward Ho: Removal of the Ohio Shawnees, 1832–1833." *Bulletin of the Historical and Philosophical Society of Ohio* 15 (January 1957).

Kvasnicka, Robert M. "George Manypenny," in Robert M. Kvasnicka and Herman J. Viola, eds., *The Commissioners of Indian Affairs, 1824–1977.* Lincoln: University of Nebraska Press, 1979.

Malin, James C. "Indian Policy and Westward Expansion." *Bulletin of the University of Kansas Humanistic Studies* 2 (1921).

———. "The Motives of Stephen A. Douglas in the Organization of Nebraska Territory: A Letter Dated December 17, 1853." *Kansas Historical Quarterly* 19 (November 1951).

McCluggage, Robert W. "The Senate and Indian Land Titles, 1800–1825." *Western Historical Quarterly* 1, no. 4 (October 1970).

McKee, Howard I. "The Platte Purchase." *Missouri Historical Review* 32, no. 2 (January 1938).

"Mission to the Great Osages." *Missionary Herald* 18 (January 1822).

"Mission to the Osages." *Missionary Herald* 17 (January 1821).

"The Osages." *Missionary Herald* 22 (January 1826).

Parsons, Lynn Hudson. "'A Perpetual Harrow upon My Feelings': John Quincy Adams and the American Indian." *New England Quarterly* 46, no. 3 (September 1973).

Prucha, Francis Paul. "Indian Removal and the Great American Desert." *Indiana Magazine of History* 59, no. 4 (December 1963).

Ronda, James P. "'We Have a Country': Race, Geography, and the Invention of Indian Territory." *Journal of the Early Republic* 19, no. 3 (Fall 1999).

Socolofsky, Homer E. "Wyandot Floats." *Kansas Historical Quarterly* 36 (Autumn 1970).

Trennert, Robert A., Jr. "The Mormons and the Office of Indian Affairs: The Conflict over Winter Quarters, 1846–1852." *Nebraska History* 53, no. 3 (Fall 1972).

Unrau, William E. "The Civil War Career of Jesse Henry Leavenworth." *Montana: The Magazine of Western History* 12, no. 2 (Spring 1961).

———. "The Council Grove Merchants and the Kansa Indians, 1855–1870." *Kansas Historical Quarterly* 24, no. 3 (Autumn 1968).

———. "The Depopulation of the Dhegiha-Siouan Kansas Prior to Removal." *New Mexico Historical Review* 48, no. 2 (October 1973).

———. "Fur Trader and Indian Office Obstruction to Smallpox Vaccination in the St. Louis Indian Superintendency, 1831–1834." *Plains Anthropologist* 34 (May 1989).

———. "George C. Sibley's Plea for the 'Garden of Missouri' in 1824." *Missouri Historical Society Bulletin* 17, no. 1 (October 1970).

Van Meter McCoy, Sondra. "Central Kansas Trading Ranches on the Santa Fe Trail," in Leo E. Oliva, ed., *Adventure on the Santa Fe Trail.* Topeka: Kansas State Historical Society, 1988.

Wilhelm, Paul, Duke of Wuerttenberg. "First Journey to North America in the Years 1822–1824." Translated by William G. Beck. *South Dakota Historical Collections* 19 (1938).

Maps

"Indian Country." Supplement, *National Geographic* 207, no. 4 (September 2004).

Theses

Ast, Kevin B. "Divided We Stand: Osage Leadership before Removal." M.A. thesis, Wichita State University, 1991.

Damron, Gary N. "The Friends Missionary Establishment among the Shawnee Indians in Kansas." M.A. thesis, Wichita State University, 1985.

Keckeisen, Robert Joseph. "The Kansa 'Half-Breed' Lands: Contravention and Transformation of United States Indian Policy in Kansas." M.A. thesis, Wichita State University, 1977.

Index